GW01465690

MAKING SENSE OF COMMUNITY

by Victoria Nash
with Ian Christie

ippr

ippr

30-32 Southampton Street, London WC2E 7RA
Tel: 020 7470 6100 Fax: 020 7470 6111
info@ippr.org.uk
www.ippr.org
Registered charity 800065

The Institute for Public Policy Research (ippr), established in 1988, is Britain's leading independent think tank on the centre left. The values that drive our work include delivering social justice, deepening democracy, increasing environmental sustainability and enhancing human rights. Through our well-researched and clearly argued policy analysis, our publications, our media events, our strong networks in government, academia and the corporate and voluntary sector, we play a vital role in maintaining the momentum of progressive thought.

ippr's aim is to bridge the political divide between the social democratic liberal traditions, the intellectual divide between the academics and the policy makers and the cultural divide between the policy-making establishment and the citizen. As an independent institute, we have the freedom to determine our research agenda. ippr has charitable status and is funded by a mixture of corporate, charitable, trade union and individual donations.

Research is ongoing, and new projects being developed, in a wide range of policy areas including sustainability, health and social care, social policy, citizenship and governance, education, economics, democracy and community, media and digital society and public private partnerships. We will shortly embark on major new projects in the fields of social justice, overseas development and democratic renewal. In 2003 we aim to grow into a permanent centre for contemporary progressive thought, recognised both at home and globally.

For further information you can contact ippr's external affairs department on info@ippr.org.uk, you can view our website at www.ippr.org and you can buy our books from central books on 0845 458 9910 or email ippr@centralbooks.com.

Trustees

Chris Powell (Chairman)	Gail Rebuck (Secretary)	Jeremy Hardie (Treasurer)
Professor Kumar Bhattacharyya	Lord Hollick	Chai Patel
Lord Brooke	Jane Humphries	Dave Prentis
Lord Eatwell	Roger Jowell	Lord Puttnam
John Edmonds	Neil Kinnock	Sir Martin Rees
Lord Gavron	Richard Lambert	Jan Royall
Chris Gibson Smith	Professor David Marquand	Ed Sweeney
Professor Anthony Giddens	Frances O'Grady	Baroness Williams
		Baroness Young of Old Scone

Production & design by **EMPHASIS**
ISBN 1 86030 205 X
© IPPR 2003

Contents

Acknowledgments
About the authors
Executive summary   i

Introduction   1

1. Contrasting experiences of community   3

2. Setting out the issues   14

3. Providing opportunities for interaction   27

4. Reassuring neighbourhoods   46

5. Building trust in governance   62

6. Mainstreaming a concern for community   73

   Conclusion   88
   References   90
   Appendix   95

Acknowledgements

IPPR would like to thank Lloyds TSB, Amey, Powergen, BUPA, the Gatsby Charitable Trust, Notting Hill Housing Trust, the Peabody Trust and Newcastle City Council for their generous support of this project. We are also grateful to Lady Dorit Young for granting us permission to use Lord Michael Young's name in the formulation of policy on 'Young Clubs'. We would also like to thank all those people whom we interviewed or spoke to in Coventry or on related issues, as without their co-operation this research would not have been possible:

David Galliers
Stella Manzie
John Payne
Jenny Venn
Miles Mackie
Rachel Flowers
Bernie Lee
Maggie Howey
John Benington
Harry Salmon
Amanda Root
Linda Gove-Evans
Tom White
Jane Hughes
Tony Sewell
Andy Bannister
Bill Hall
WATCH management committee
Farid Noor
Fay & Area Co-ordination South-West
Pat Walsh
John White
Penny Walker
Katrina Goldie
Carol Finn
Mylene Feeney
Huw Jones

Ian Roxburgh
Brett Willers
Vicki Urch
Helen Shankster
Ann McLauchlan
Janice Nichols
Sue Darling
Polly Dickinson
Babs Haye
Mike Geddes
Margaret Dieterman
Rosalyn Johnson
Duncan Elliott
Howard Cook
Pete Longdon
Steve Graham
Linda Rowatt
Dave at the GAP café
Dorothy Senior
David Lloyd
Hazel White
Asha Bhardwaj
Linda Brewster
Jane Powell
Jenny Bolfe
Leslie Williams

and all who took part in the focus groups.

About the authors

Dr Victoria Nash was a Research Fellow at ippr, leading a programme of research for the Communities Initiative. She is now Policy and Research Officer at the Oxford Internet Institute and is also a Lecturer in Politics for Trinity College, Oxford. Her previous publications include *Reclaiming Community* (ippr 2002) and *Any Volunteers for the Good Society* (ippr 2002, edited with Will Paxton).

Ian Christie is an independent researcher and consultant on sustainable development, and is an Associate Director of The Local Futures Group and www.opendemocracy.net. He has recently co-authored books such as *Putting Community at the Heart of Development* (Green Issues Ltd 2002) and *Managing Sustainable Development* (Earthscan 2000).

Executive summary

> Community is the governing idea of modern social democracy…a key task for our second term is to develop greater coherence around our commitment to community (Blair 2002).

Since coming to power in 1997, one defining characteristic of Labour's policy agenda has been its stated commitment to the value of community. This is apparent not just in the language of policy such as the 'New Deal for Communities' but in the actual substance of initiatives which has seen, for example, sums of money set aside for supporting local groups (community 'capacity-building') and a Treasury cross-cutting spending review set up to examine the adequacy of current spending on public spaces. Similarly, the establishment of units such as the Social Exclusion Unit, the Neighbourhood Renewal Unit and the Community Cohesion Unit means that there are now departments of government actually charged with monitoring and improving the quality of people's social relationships, whether this be as a way of relieving poverty or reducing cultural tensions.

This policy focus is long overdue. Community – the character and quality of the local social relationships where we live – clearly has a significant impact on our quality of life. Put most simply, none of us want to fear our neighbours, and many appreciate the basic resources such as information, support or 'cups of sugar' that they can, on occasion, provide. This report argues that although the Government's record on issues of community is a significant advance, there is still some way to go, both in joining up thinking on key issues, and in addressing quite fundamental problems. It is also true that most of the Government's efforts at supporting community have so far been targeted at the most excluded, when the health of local social ties really matters to all.

Community of place

Many different sorts of ties are described as community relationships, and in our increasingly mobile, electronic, individualistic lives, community of place can sound like an out-dated or nostalgic ideal. But for lots of people whose family or friends live nearby, this is still a vivid reality, whilst for others who are tied to a locality in virtue of parenting responsibilities, lack of income or age, there is little choice to be had in where or with whom they socialise. Even the wealthy can choose their neighbourhood but not their neighbours, and ultimately, all of us will be affected if community breaks down. The tensions and riots that broke out in Bradford, Burnley and Oldham in 2001 should stand as a stark reminder of the extent to which our quality of life could be affected when trust and respect decay.

Although community of place does thus have an impact on everyone's personal well-being, this report recognises that for many, local social ties are not the most meaningful or emotionally close. As a consequence, this report works with a 'thinner' notion of community than might be expected. Any such definition must capture what kind of social relationships government should legitimately protect and support for all. For our purposes community of place is understood to comprise 'A rich variety of social ties, all of a minimally trusting and civil nature, where those ties are grounded in a shared commitment to place'.

Public policy already has an impact on community. Housing policy affects who lives next to whom, planning and development regulations determine what places to meet are available, whilst policy on crime will affect how safe our streets feel. The argument in this report, then, starts from the premise that if public policy is going to affect the quality of our local social relationships, it should at least do no harm, and wherever possible, it should try to do some good. Despite the current government's good intentions, on this point there is still some way yet to go.

Impact on real communities

The impact of policy on community is most easily observed through the eyes of real people in real neighbourhoods. Three case study areas in Coventry helped us to identify where policies have had positive and detrimental effects. The three localities studied were Earlsdon, Canley and Hillfields, chosen as neighbourhoods with very different social and economic conditions. The report is written as an ethnographic study, with issues seen through the perspective of these neighbourhoods and the people we spoke to there. Over the course of eight months we carried out focus groups with local residents, interviewed a wide range of stakeholders and spent time simply getting to know the areas. Such a holistic approach enabled us to think about the component parts of 'community' and the policies which have an effect on these parts. In order to ensure that policy thinking on community is joined up effectively in the future, public authorities should try to determine how their decisions and practice affect:

● Opportunities for interaction: healthy social ties will only develop where people have the chance to meet and mingle and live out a vigorous public life;

● The 'feel' of a neighbourhood: no matter how many high-quality public spaces or communal services there are, if a neighbourhood feels insecure and unsafe, people will not leave their houses to enjoy them;

● Patterns of trust between residents, or between residents and the public authorities that serve them: interaction will not build trust if the experience is negative or unpleasant.

The potential and limits of policy

Although government could do much more to support community of place, there are important structural limitations which will dramatically affect what sorts of social relationships develop in different areas. Poverty and economic polarisation, for example, will always put pressure on social relations between different income groups whilst work and regional trends mean that some dormitory towns will be almost empty during the day. It also has to be accepted that government cannot make us trust each other or force us to interact. As such, none of the recommendations are guaranteed to build community. What they will do, though, is provide the elements of a supportive policy framework, within which the development of social ties or the growth of trust should be possible.

Our research has shown that there are several key policy areas which have a particularly important effect on community. These areas are:

● Planning and development

● Provision for young people

● Crime reduction and policing

● Design and liveability of the public realm

● Methods of frontline service delivery.

Getting policy 'right' on these issues will go a long way towards providing a supportive framework for community. The remaining sections of this summary show how.

Opportunities for interaction

Community of place refers to the relationships between people living in a particular area. Those relationships may be close and friendly, or they may be weak and anonymous. In order for us to talk about 'community of place' at all, though, there must be some sort of public life to an area: places where people can pass, mingle or even meet. No social ties at all will be established if people remain in the privacy of their own homes: some sort of public places must be provided where people can interact, whether this be safe streets and open spaces or shops, pubs and cafés. Apart from the economic disparities, the most obvious difference between Earlsdon and the other two areas studied was the range of public amenities available in that neighbourhood. Earlsdon residents have on their doorstep not just a wide range of shops and green spaces, but also their own theatre, a grand municipal library and several pubs, restaurants and coffee shops. Both Canley and Hillfields lack important amenities, and in the former, this lack is exacerbated by the area's distance from the city centre. It is clearly hard for there to be any public life in a neighbourhood which lacks a range of public spaces. Certainly streets are public spaces too, but people need a reason to use them. If there are almost no local facilities, as in Canley, then the only time people will use the streets is to get into their cars or wait for public transport to take them elsewhere.

We found that three policy areas had a particularly significant effect on the range of spaces and places available locally for interaction. Those were planning and development, provision of facilities for young people, and the range of policies that affect social mix.

Planning and development

Planning policy clearly has an impact here, simply by regulating what can be built where and how. Our research showed that policy on planning and regulation can have a particularly significant effect on the availability of spaces and places where people can meet in four key ways:

- By regulating housing density of new developments

- By determining the number and location of congregational spaces

- By the methods used to deal with massive demand for new housing in the south-east

- By permitting or not permitting the development of 'gated' communities.

There are several ways in which changes could be made to planning and regulation policy which would help to support a richer variety of public spaces and places where people can meet. Amongst the most important ideas might be:

- Regular audits of 'congregational spaces' in each neighbourhood to be conducted by local authorities to determine how much such space is available and what condition it is in. This information could then be used to inform planning decisions, or public spending decisions.

- An 'Investor in Community' badge to be awarded and monitored by CABE. This would be awarded to commercial developers pursuing design policies which fully reflect the principles of sustainable development through the integration of economic, social and environmental factors in design and implementation. Public procurement of new homes and other dwellings should exclude developers not achieving this standard.

Provision of amenities for young people

It was clear in all three areas that there is a distinct lack of facilities for young people and that, as a consequence, many are observed simply 'hanging around' on the streets and in public places. This is increasingly seen as threatening behaviour which results in other age groups (particularly the elderly) refraining from using these spaces. In the interests of supporting community, it is therefore important to make suitable provision for young people in order to ensure that the public realm is well used and that barriers are not created between different age groups. The current framework of provision for young people (via the Youth Service and Connexions) is not necessarily well-placed to rectify the situation, as neither of these can offer significant capital investment and both adopt a more education- rather than leisure-based approach. Improving the leisure options available to young people should help to make streets and public spaces seem less threatening, and in order to achieve that:

- Partnerships should be established within local authorities between youth workers, leisure development officers, community development workers and parks/open spaces officers to arrive at a strategy of leisure provision for young people. This mode of working would fit well within the Connexions framework which stresses partnership working but currently lacks a significant focus on leisure.

- A programme of capital investment for the development or construction of 'Young Clubs' – a programme for revitalising youth club provision and other facilities for youth – should be introduced in all areas eligible for Neighbourhood Renewal funding, and possibly extended at a later date. Both new money and new thinking is required to transform the existing image and plant of youth clubs which have often been allowed to decay. It would be essential for young people to be involved in the design, development and management of these facilities to ensure that they meet real needs and are not seen as another instrument of authority.

Social mix

It may seem odd to talk about social mix as a way of creating opportunities for interaction, but it is essential if we try to answer the question of 'interaction between whom?'. One of the challenges in supporting community is the need to find ways of ensuring that different social groups do not come to lead entirely separate and effectively segregated lives at the local level. Without such integration tensions may arise and it is unlikely that all groups will feel themselves to have an equally secure place in public life. Social mix is also a valuable social resource as it allows networks to be built between different groups such that goods, information and opportunities are effectively passed on. This might mean mixing age groups, ethnic groups or income groups. Of the three areas we studied, only Hillfields scored well in terms of ethnic heterogeneity. The current wisdom in policy-making is that social mix is something brought about in the spheres of housing or education, but our analysis shows that there is good reason to focus on other environments where people would voluntarily mix. In particular there is good reason to look at activities such as sport, leisure and the arts as ways of encouraging interaction between different social groups. These are all activities that people undertake for the sheer enjoyment of doing them, and they may not mind so much with whom they do them. Sport is also a very effective way of getting people to co-operate through teamwork, and as such is a valuable tool in the process of integration. New communication technologies also offer potentially exciting opportunities for helping diversity thrive. Government and public bodies could do more to encourage and support social mix:

- As major funders of sports, leisure and the arts, the Community Fund, NOF, Sports England and the Arts Council should co-ordinate work on developing new programmes of funding specifically for leisure, sports and arts projects which support diversity and the integration of different social groups. Sport England could also run an ambassadorship scheme helping local teams and key sporting figures to champion projects which support diversity and integration (such as the successful Football Unites, Racism Divides scheme.)

- Given the already encouraging results of some studies, more research is needed into the potential of computer-mediated communication to promote interaction between residents of different social groups, particularly in new housing developments. To aid this process, and to encourage social integration, government-supported developments such as Millennium Villages could incorporate easy-to-use computer-mediated communication such as neighbourhood e-mail networks and intranets.

Reassuring neighbourhoods

Although it is essential that localities manifest a wide range of public spaces and amenities where people can mingle in the public realm, they will be unwilling to use these spaces if the area feels threatening. In order to support community at the local level, policy must therefore ensure that neighbourhoods are reassuring places to move around.

Of the areas we studied, both Canley and Hillfields suffered from crime and anti-social behaviour to some degree, and in both cases residents said that this created a feeling of insecurity and would discourage them from using certain parts of the neighbourhood. In reality though, reassurance is about more than just the absence of crime or the fear of crime. The quality of the public environment and its design play an important role in how secure we feel. Similarly, the quantity and speed of traffic in an area will encourage or discourage people from using local amenities and public spaces. In order to ensure that localities feel reassuring, then, government must do more to address each of these issues.

Liveability

Graffiti, vandalism, litter and decay may not affect our safety but they do combine to make an area feel insecure. Design is also crucial not just in the obvious sense that certain layouts of buildings, streets and alleyways provide more places to hide, but also in the sense that open, well-overlooked, mixed-use spaces are naturally reassuring. Bare windowless walls and the absence of the natural bustle that guarantees 'eyes on the street' will provide no protection for passers-by. These issues have been described as the factors that makes spaces more or less 'liveable', and the UK government has recently embraced the liveability agenda, recognising the impact these factors can have on our quality of life. However more can yet be done:

- More crime prevention money should be directed towards 'positive' measures which defend public space by designing the built environment to encourage constant use, rather than currently dominant 'defensive' strategies such as installing CCTV which do little to make crime harder to commit. Initiatives targeting say design or lighting in the public realm could actively encourage more use of public space which naturally provides more 'eyes on the street'. CABE should work with local authorities, NACRO and the Home Office to research and develop such a strategy.

- Local authorities are charged with drawing up Community Plans promoting the long-term welfare of their areas. The process should include the creation, based on genuine consultation with residents, of 'public realm strategies' as recommended by the Urban Task Force, with plans looking up to twenty years ahead. The quality of public space – the streetscape, parks, green spaces – should be focused upon by Local Strategic Partnerships set up to oversee the process of neighbourhood renewal in disadvantaged localities.

Traffic patterns

Traffic density and speed can have three important effects on local social relations. First, the car is a private space, and those travelling by car do not have to interact with others. Secondly, areas where there is lower car use may well support a wider range of local amenities that will, as in Hillfields, attract users on foot. Thirdly, as has been shown in several classic studies, car use discourages socialising, in the sense that streets with heavy traffic do not make talking or playing in the street an attractive idea. We would consequently recommend that:

- Local authorities should make the planning and implementation of Home Zones and 20mph zones in residential areas a priority.

Crime and anti-social behaviour

The impact of crime and anti-social behaviour on community should be quite obvious, and judging by the recent introduction of measures such as Anti-Social Behaviour Orders (ASBOs) and changes outlined in the policing White Paper, it is an impact that the Government is all too aware of. It was clear from studying the three neighbourhoods in Coventry, however, that more needs to be done, and that in particular, existing measures for dealing with anti-social behaviour are inadequate. Discussions with senior police officers also made it clear that there are institutional barriers which now make it harder to carry out good community policing than in the past. These barriers need to be addressed. We therefore recommend that:

- The scale of Key Performance Indicators and national objectives for policing should be reassessed, and alternative systems considered. A possible alternative might be assessment according to local objectives set by forces themselves in conjunction with Crime and Disorder Reduction Partnerships and significant involvement of local residents.

- More research to help identify effective methods of preventing or dealing with anti-social behaviour, looking at the effects of the wider policy framework as well as strategies which might avoid recourse to the courts.

Building trust in governance

As well as seeking to promote contact and trust *between residents*, we need to acknowledge that healthy community relations require at least a moderate degree of trust *in authority*. Without this, there is a danger that a neighbourhood might become very inward-looking and defensive, and that it might be unable to make the most of resources available to it through public agencies. Just as a framework for inter-personal contact and trust can be provided by pursuing some of the recommendations outlined above, so an improved framework for institutional trust can be developed if certain changes are made to the way public agencies operate. Hillfields residents appeared to experience better, more trusting relations with local services and their political representatives than residents in the other two areas. A key component of this seemed to be that key public figures were well embedded in the area itself, and that as such they were perceived to understand the area's needs more effectively. We looked more closely at three contexts in which public bodies and local residents inter-relate.

Front-line service delivery

Unsurprisingly we found that residents in Earlsdon rarely had any direct contact with public servants other than teachers or doctors. Residents in Hillfields and Canley on the other hand had plenty of contact, and they were quite clear as to what might make them trust public bodies more. In both areas there was a strong feeling that the professionals and managers they dealt with had no real understanding of their needs or experiences. None of the council officers, police, teachers or other professionals we spoke to lived in either of these areas. The importance of 'empathy' was also highlighted in our study of an effective third-sector employment service operating in Hillfields. Here, clients felt that the service was successful precisely because advisors knew what it was like to be unemployed. Recommendations that might promote a more understanding approach by public servants could include:

- Extensive 'capacity-building' training to be given to all new MPs, councillors and members of LSPs, involving regular visits to local areas and in particular to the worst-off ones, and frequent contact with residents' groups. MPs, councillors and professional members of key local partnerships should spend at least a short amount of time living in the areas they represent. Frontline service deliverers such as teachers, police and housing officers dealing with particular areas should also undergo an induction process which familiarises them with the area, with key local figures and an understanding of local issues.

- More effort should be made to foster, train and recruit frontline service staff from the localities in which services operate, for example, in housing and employment services. Support and incentives should be available to encourage public servants such as teachers, doctors and policemen to move into the areas they serve.

Public involvement

Public involvement and consultation have been pursued by the current government apparently as a way of reinventing the relationship between citizens and public services. Despite this noble ideal, poorly run consultation and involvement strategies will not build trust but destroy it. Several residents in the Hillfields area felt very let down by one service provider who had, they felt, undertaken a recent consultation process in an unfair way. Whether this is the case or not, the example highlights the dangers of poorly thought-out public involvement strategies and makes it all the more imperative that in areas such as Canley, where institutional trust is very low, such processes are only undertaken with a great deal of forethought and careful communication.

Political representatives

Very few people in the areas studied could even name their councillors, let alone express trust in them. The one exception was again in Hillfields where several residents spoke in glowing terms about their representatives. Here the difference appeared to be, once again, local experience and empathic understanding; the candidates referred to not only live in the area but make many house visits to residents and are well-recognised local figures. It was also seen as important that neither of these candidates belonged to a mainstream party, which supposedly gave them more reason to focus on local issues and needs. This perception has potentially devastating implications for mainstream parties trying very hard to reduce voter apathy in local elections. In this light we recommend that:

●   More research on the connection between local party structure and perceptions of representatives' legitimacy should be undertaken in order to help us understand what is needed both to stimulate effective local leadership and to re-engage voters in local democracy.

Mainstreaming a concern for community

There is a danger that all the preceding recommendations will just be seen as a piecemeal approach to the challenge of supporting community. Whilst each of these recommendations, taken individually, would help, they are really just presented as examples of what a more community-friendly approach would require. In an ideal world, policy-makers would just intuitively understand that certain types of action could undermine community of place. The suggestion is that, although in many ways it should just be common sense that certain policy actions will undermine community, a more methodical form of assessment might help uncover these effects. As part of our research we considered two possible approaches, one which involved assessing the impact of policies on community after their introduction, perhaps through the use of indicators. There appeared to be strong reasons for not taking this approach.

An alternative strategy would involve 'proofing' policy in advance, testing any policy proposals against a set of criteria that could help to identify where trade-offs between goals of community and other policy goals might need to be made. Thus we might, for example ask whether a proposed policy would erect physical barriers between different groups or foster conflict between them, whether it would undermine the quality of existing public space or if it would erode local pride. We think that a community-proofing tool could help to mainstream a concern for community in the policy-making process and as such we recommend that:

- This community-proofing approach should be refined further in a series of pilots, to be undertaken in a variety of communities, affluent and less well-off, by a range of organisations such as:
  - Local authorities, in developing community plans;
  - Neighbourhood renewal partnerships, in developing regeneration programmes and projects;
  - Property developers and planners, in assessing the impact of proposed new housing developments;
  - Local Strategic Partnerships, in assessing long-term scenarios arising from diverse visions of how their areas could develop;
  - Faith communities, in assessing proposals for the introduction of faith-based schools.

Taken together, the framework for analysis and recommendations laid out in this report should make it clear that much can be done to support community, improving quality of life and preventing the misery of community breakdown. This will often be possible not only in ways that do not conflict with existing policy goals, but in ways that actually serve to reinforce them. As such it is a pressing case.

Introduction

This report is concerned with a vital aspect of the idea of 'community': community of place. It starts from the premise that even if the neighbourhood is not the source of our most emotionally close relationships, the quality and character of local social relations can have a significant impact on our quality of life, and as such it is something that policy-makers should care about. This research project was set up to establish what impact public policy can and does have on the quality of local social relations. We wanted to identify where public policy could do more to support community at the local level. Although policy-makers can never force us to interact or trust each other, they can provide a framework within which trust and interaction might flourish. The following chapters are an attempt to identify what such a framework might look like.

Although 'community' may sound like an unproblematically good thing, it is a term that is notoriously hard to define, and one which, in some academic circles, is often regarded as potentially sinister and 'exclusionary'. The interim report of IPPR's Communities Initiative, *Reclaiming Community*, attempted to address some of these issues, establishing what we might mean by community of place and whether academic suspicion of the term could be squared with its policy relevance (Nash 2002). Rather than appealing to nostalgic visions of close-knit communities, bound by family and history, we tried to identify what sort of local social relations most citizens could aspire to in this day and age. In that report we argued that community of place mattered most obviously in the simple sense that none of us want to live somewhere where we fear our neighbours. Most of us want to live somewhere that feels reassuring, where other residents behave in a civil and tolerant way. The other important elements of community of place were identified as a minimal sense of common identity, and a rich and diverse arrangement of social ties. The rationale for the inclusion of these elements will be explained at greater length in Chapter 2, but for current purposes it is important just to note what this report means when it refers to community (of place). In our view, the vision of local community that public policy should promote would be:

> A rich and diverse array of social ties of a trusting and civil nature, grounded in a basic shared commitment to the local neighbourhood or area.

Given the subject matter of this research project, we decided to look at the impact of policy on community through the eyes of particular people and places. Academic study of social networks and their features has become a highly technical subject, but we wanted to know about the subjective feel of areas rather than just their objective social structure. In particular, we wanted to know what makes an area feel reassuring, what sorts of factors make people more or less likely to interact with their neighbours, what encourages or discourages civil behaviour or trust, and on each of these points, we wanted to know what impact public policy could have. To answer these questions, it was clear that some sort of empirical study was needed. For this reason we undertook an in-depth qualitative study of three very different neighbourhoods in a single city, Coventry.

In the tradition of the rich and enduring community studies of post-war Britain, such as those undertaken by Michael Young and Peter Wilmott, the method we used was ethnographic and descriptive (Wilmott & Young 1957; 1960). As well as carrying out standard focus groups and interviews, we also spent time in the areas, walking and talking in all parts of the neighbourhoods, observing as much as possible and hearing from residents what it is like to live there. In the course of the research we spoke to over a hundred people, and got to know all parts of the areas studied.

We have chosen to write this report in an ethnographic style, making the most of the rich information we acquired. The first chapter offers a description of those three areas. The hope is that the very different social, physical and economic character of these areas will become vivid and that the policy issues arising should seem obvious and pressing. These policy questions will then be discussed at greater length in the later chapters of the book.

1. Contrasting experiences of community

I feel Hillfields has quite a pleasant community spirit. A few years ago it was bad but I really think the community themselves are pulling together and doing something about it. (Long-term resident, Hillfields)

It's a containable community, it has a history of good community but sadly that's in the past. (New resident, Canley)

It has a strong community spirit compared to other areas of the city...it is like a village. (Long-term resident, Earlsdon)

Coventry is a city divided along a north-south axis. The more affluent middle-class residential areas such as Earlsdon and Stivichall are to the south of the city centre, opening up around the commuter corridor of the road connecting Leamington Spa to the city, thus separated from the old industrial north. But the contrast between north and south is more than just economically stark. Coventry's 1998 Community Plan reported a ten-year difference in average life expectancy between wealthier areas such as Earlsdon and some of the poorest neighbourhoods around the north side of the city, a gap that the Council is trying hard to close. In general, there is a marked variation between neighbourhoods; remarkably different living environments and life experiences are fenced apart by single roads or railway lines. It was partly because of the obvious contrasts that we spent time in Coventry, in Earlsdon, Hillfields and Canley, trying to understand how community life differs between localities.

Earlsdon

It was originally built as an artists' quarter. It's on higher ground, so it got cleaner air...it was called the village and definitely does retain some separate identity. (New resident, Earlsdon)

The recent arrival of a national newsagent chain store appears to have upset some Earlsdon residents. Such stores are seen as a threat to the livelihood of small local retailers clustering around the natural high street, Earlsdon Street. More than this though, the chain-store image simply does not fit in. Earlsdon is a classic example of the 'urban village', and residents are very keen to keep it that way. Precisely what makes the area distinctive, they feel, is the range of very local amenities, run by local residents and often staffed by people who know the area and recognise familiar faces:

'You hear the butcher talking to people and using their first name...that adds to the sense of community spirit'.

The neighbourhood is well served by small shops and businesses. The high street is a thriving, bustling place, lined not just by shops and banks, but by restaurants, cafés, picture galleries, and, (providing a truly middle class stamp), a delicatessen and an organic food shop. At almost any time of day there is movement and bustle on this street, in sharp contrast to the sleepy Victorian terraces that form a surrounding grid. This clearly matters to local residents who told us:

> *What I like about Earlsdon is that it is always busy, people walking round...where I used to live in Coundon you can walk down the road and not see anyone – it has not got that community feel about it.*

> *I had to go round the corner to get a pint of milk, it took me three quarters of an hour because of all the people I stopped to talk to.*

It is certainly true that Earlsdon displays an impressively strong local identity. All the residents we spoke to were very keen to tell us how distinctive the area felt compared to anywhere else in Coventry. It was variously depicted as friendlier, safer, more stable, better served, even happier. The area's amenities, its sense of community, its appearance: all these things were said to set Earlsdon apart from other neighbourhoods in the city.

The area also has several very obvious landmarks. These include the roundabout just below the shop-lined Earlsdon Street where main roads in and out of the area meet. On top of that roundabout sits an old clock tower, recently renovated thanks to the generosity of local businesses. To the right is the Library (a fine old redbrick municipal building) and next to that the much sought-after Earlsdon Primary. To the left of the roundabout is the Methodist Church (the site of Scouts meetings, toddler groups and a new part-time coffee shop). All of these civic spaces were described by various people as helping to define Earlsdon's identity, and well they might, for even to an outsider it is clear that this solid and well-maintained public realm provides opportunities for a vigorous public and community life.

As well as providing many opportunities for local residents to meet one another, Earlsdon also seems to provide a fairly reassuring environment for people to interact in. It feels safe to walk around: even alleyways did not feel threatening or oppressive. Several people said they are happy to walk around at night. This was reiterated by residents who said that it 'feels quite safe compared to other places in the city', whilst others praised what they felt to be a high police presence. The physical environment is undoubtedly another important factor. As most of the terraced houses front directly onto the road, or have only a small garden at the front, there is a reassuring feeling that the street is overlooked and safe, a feeling which is further reinforced by the fact that many of the houses have large windows and that there is plenty of street lighting.

This reassuring atmosphere seemed to support, and is perhaps strengthened by, a tendency for Earlsdon people to trust their fellow residents. Most said that they would be happy to leave a key with their neighbours whilst away. Plenty of examples were given as to ways in which neighbours helped each other: 'the man next door takes out the wheelie bins, the man across the road cuts the hedge'. This rather rosy-hued account was tempered somewhat, though, by the more realistic view that despite all this philanthropic behaviour, neighbours were unlikely to be good friends, but rather just familiar people who could provide useful services: 'they're friendly enough, but I wouldn't say I go out drinking with them or anything'. This reinforces the view that local social relations are important not because they're necessarily the most meaningful or emotionally deep, but because they provide useful services and can strongly affect our quality of life, especially when things turn sour.

Time spent in Earlsdon thus does much to dispel the myth that the middle classes do not value community. When we asked focus group members what were the 'pluses' of living in Earlsdon, almost every one mentioned either the 'sense of community', the friendliness or the feeling of safety. There was a recognition that some people in particular did a great deal to support community networks and identity. There is a neighbourhood newspaper, the *Echo*, renowned for publicising important local issues and news. An annual festival has traditionally been held on the high street, although due to its size it moved to the Common for the first time this year. Local shops and businesses were also seen as looking after the interests of the area, if only because it was ultimately in their interests to do so.

The extent to which residents appeared to trust their local retailers was emphasised by surprising claims that rather than go to the Council with local problems, residents would seek support from these businesses: 'If I had a burning issue about something I would either write to the Echo to get people to back the cause or go to local shop keepers' said one person. Another complained that 'People in the shops, you can get to know them and relate to them; with the local council I haven't got a clue'.

Such views, of course, reflect the fact that in an affluent area such as Earlsdon, residents have little contact with Council officers, and that familiarity and understanding are essential in building trust. For Council officers or Members to be trusted in this same way, it seemed that they would have to display far more local knowledge and be seen to make more of a commitment to the area. As one resident put it, 'They (the council) would have to come out and meet you and come into the area more, make themselves more well-known.'

That Earlsdon residents enjoy such healthy community relations must be due, in large part, to the relative ease of local life. The area is reasonably affluent, with an average income of £24,570 per head and unemployment of just 2.5 per cent. Average life expectancy is 79.2 years and crime figures are relatively low, with the biggest problems being retail fraud and shoplifting at the retail park near the station (Coventry City Council 2002). Earlsdon is a largely white and middle class neighbourhood. A couple of younger residents listed this lack of diversity amongst the more negative aspects of the locality, but it is unlikely that this will change dramatically in the near future. Indeed, there is already resistance to the influx of 'outsiders' who are attracted in to use the pubs and attend the festival. There is very little social housing in Earlsdon, with the rental sector being dominated by private lets, most often to students. There is thus a good mix of age groups, which does help to stabilise the area, but there are few people on low incomes or from ethnic minorities.

A local health-worker noted that there was a more negative side to Earlsdon's apparently healthy community relations. Having worked for some time with new mothers, this nurse told us that she had seen a great deal of isolation in the area. Many of the women she dealt with had previously worked full-time and found the transition to motherhood difficult. Although they may have numerous friendly relationships with their neighbours, what many of these women apparently lack is peer-group support. If this insight is accurate, then we need to take a more nuanced view of Earlsdon's community relationships: plenty of casual 'weak ties' perhaps, but maybe a relative lack of the stronger more supportive relationships that are helpful in times of transition or stress.

Although basic economic factors do undoubtedly make a difference, it is still hard to identify why local social relationships are as positive as they are. Earlsdon's history and origins no doubt makes a difference, as must the key local figures who keep the newspaper, the annual festival and local trade alive. Another factor could simply be the layout of the area and the quality of the environment. The absence of graffiti, vandalism and litter, the high-density terraced housing with their sociable gardens, the number of high-quality green spaces and beautiful parks: all make Earlsdon a pleasant and reassuring place to live, and people try hard to keep it that way.

Hillfields

You make friends very quickly here. You only need to go to a shop a couple of times. (New resident, Hillfields)

Philips hardware store in Hillfields was established in 1915, and has been run as a family business ever since. Winston Churchill once ordered some greenhouse goods from there and the store still supplies customers all over Britain and even overseas. Showing me the original faded equivalent of today's 'Yellow Pages', the elderly current owner of the store told me there used to be more than 30 ironmongers in

Coventry in 1939, including several others in the Hillfields area. Now just a few remain and mass retailers such as B&Q and Homebase deal with the bulk of the trade. The secret to Philips' survival, we were told, was specialisation and expertise; the store offers a staggering range of specialist hardware products and employs and retains approachable and knowledgeable staff.

The Winston Churchill anecdote is important because it illustrates one successful strategy for attracting people into an area that suffers from the problem of stigmatisation, namely providing specialist business which can offer services found nowhere else in a city or region. Hillfields needs more such businesses: it is a relatively poor area, and despite its proximity to the city centre it feels very enclosed. It has been the target of regeneration efforts since the Community Development Programme of the 1970s; on measures such as unemployment, average life expectancy and average income, the area is still performing badly. Despite this, local residents display an infectious optimism and there is evidence of excellent work being done to build the social capital that will reinforce the effects of financial investment to boost the area's fortunes. There is a real sense, expressed in our interviews and focus groups, that for Hillfields, the worst is over, and recovery is on the way.

Hillfields, like Earlsdon, is very close to the city centre. It sprawls out from under the ring road to the north-west of the city, naturally bounded on all sides by roads and the Coventry Canal. The main route into the area, up Primrose Hill Street, is dominated by a cluster of 1960s tower blocks on the left-hand side. This road, which is the effective high street for Hillfields, has recently been developed to ensure that first impressions are as positive as possible. Old shops have been knocked down to allow for the construction of attractive redbrick housing, whilst smart official signage informs visitors of the current regeneration plans and shows how things are improving. At the top of this street is a brand new village square, which doubles most of the time as a car park, but which does at least provide residents with a space to hang around. Despite the high visibility of Hillfields' tower blocks, most of the area's housing is traditional Victorian and Edwardian terraced redbrick. The houses are smaller than their equivalent in Earlsdon, but most are well-maintained 'two-up, two-down' homes.

There is a definite sense of local identity and community in Hillfields that is obvious to an outsider. That identity has been largely forged around a sense of 'siege', the feeling that Hillfields was dealt a very poor hand, and that other areas of the city were only too happy to stand by and watch it go under. Typical comments were 'part of what makes the community spirit is because there are so many local important issues, everyone has very strong opinions on them' and 'we see the truth as opposed to the image and think, damn, I'm going to put this right and stand up for it.' There is still great antipathy towards the local media, which residents see as adding to the area's poor reputation by exaggerating reports of crime or focusing unduly on the long-standing problem of prostitution on the streets.

Architecture, too, is felt to be a source of the distrust and suspicion with which the area is regarded; 'part of the problem is that if you say to people in the city "Hillfields", their immediate vision is of the tower blocks...until they (the housing association) decide what to do with the tower blocks, the area can't move forward, it's a real stumbling block.' Ironically, these tower blocks are regarded by local residents with a fair amount of affection, and certainly many of those who live inside them are very happy with their accommodation.

Although Hillfields' local identity may at root be defensive, the networks of local social ties that have developed from this are admirably strong and diverse. Community relationships are forged in Hillfields by two routes. First there are the loose ties built through casual encounters, meeting as neighbours, in shops or via school and children. Residents told us that it was relatively easy to build up a large network of acquaintances in Hillfields, even though the area lacks the expansive selection of shops and amenities to be found in Earlsdon. There is a plethora of corner shops, Halal butchers and fast food joints but only one place to sit and eat – the new charity-run Gap Café – and almost no truly 'neutral' meeting places not identified with a *section* of the community. One reason why it is so easy to meet people, despite the relative lack of local amenities, is perhaps because car ownership is low. As one resident said, 'in a normal area where people use a car to travel, it does not facilitate relationships.'

The second way in which local community ties are built is through the active capacity-building work of organisations such as WATCH (Working Actively To Change Hillfields). This impressive grassroots not-for-profit regeneration company provides valuable community development support for local groups, as well as highly regarded employment services. The staff are trusted and effective, and are seen as far more 'legitimate' as a provider of these services than the previous statutory equivalent. On the last count WATCH had nearly 90 local groups on their books, and there is every sign that Hillfields has a vigorous social infrastructure of self-help and support groups which are a significant resource in the turnaround of the area.

The health of Hillfields' social ties is all the more remarkable given the heterogeneity of the neighbourhood. It has a highly diverse ethnic population which is composed of recent immigrants from Eastern Europe and by long-settled Asian and Afro-Caribbean families. The 1991 census figures showed ethnic minorities to compose 36 per cent of the Hillfields population, with Indian, Pakistani and Bangladeshi groups making up most of this total. There is also a wide generational mix, perhaps somewhat distorted by the high numbers of Coventry University students living in the area. Hillfields has a very varied population and also a fluid one: the student population and the flow of asylum-seekers makes for a sizeable transient element.

The neighbourhood seems genuinely well integrated although there are concerns about isolated individuals and some families in the Bangladeshi population, and the student population is resented by some for causing problems to do with parking, noise and housing quality. The presence of asylum-seekers is generally tolerated, with only a few minor incidents occurring over the past year. This reaction seems more a result of perceived 'threatening' patterns of behaviour by young male asylum seekers, than of any inherent racism but it is too early to tell whether the issue will prove unsettling in the long term. Perhaps more interesting is the extent to which this diversity forms an important part of its identity for many local residents. They are proud to live in a generally tolerant area, and the few racially motivated comments we experienced were directed towards asylum seekers not local Asian or Afro-Caribbean residents. We heard many comments such as 'It's always been a melting pot since the sixties, it makes it a very colourful area' or 'It's always been a working class area. It can cope with anybody'.

We might not expect Hillfields to have the vibrant social character that it does. As already noted, it is not blessed with large numbers of high quality public spaces or facilities that might bring residents together. The quality of the environment is poor; residents complain about litter, dumped cars and the condoms and needles left behind by prostitutes and their clients. The area has almost no green space to speak of, and there is a problem of alcoholics congregating in the one park available. Crime levels are reasonably high, with the Council's 1999/2000 figures showing 74.9 incidents per 1000 households compared with a city average of 37.3.

But what seems clear is that people in Hillfields make their own opportunities. The strong residents' associations and plethora of community groups are evidence of people coming together and using social capital to try and improve their quality of life. Organisations such as WATCH also work effectively to create links between these different groups, ensuring that residents broaden their social ties whether this then helps them build coalitions to push for change, or simply to avoid isolation. It is also plain that many residents in Hillfields would know how to contact people in positions of influence if they needed to, most obviously through WATCH or Area Co-ordination. To our surprise, many residents were also not only able to identify their local councillors but knew how to contact them and said that they trusted them to look after the area's interests. It appeared that these councillors make a real effort to engage with residents and pursue their concerns. 'Dave Nellist and Rob Windsor...they do a lot of work for the area and are committed to it. They are not using it as a base, they are not politically motivated', we were told. It is often reported in deprived areas, that local social ties are dense but very inward-looking. Hillfields residents, however, seem to be aiming to stretch their social networks beyond the neighbourhood's boundaries.

Hillfields is an 'in-between' case in our study. Certainly it is not as cynical and untrusting as Canley, but it is a good deal 'edgier' and less tranquil than Earlsdon. Many residents we spoke to felt that it was imperative that the problems of prostitution and drug dealing were dealt with effectively. Policing is still a controversial issue, with some residents asking for a heavier police presence. CCTV cameras are much appreciated and people were generally positive about the new Neighbourhood Warden scheme in operation, even if they did not think that a warden could actually do very much if there was any trouble. Although many of the local social networks originate from a desire to change things, it might still be better if people did not have to rely on clubbing together to improve their quality of life. In more affluent areas this would certainly not be such a concern. There is thus still some way to go before Hillfields is as economically secure as Earlsdon, but it is impossible to ignore the richness of the social ties sustained in the area as a result of the problems experienced.

Canley

> *There is a spirit in Canley that needs rekindling again...over the years the council have let the area get deprived.* (Long-term resident, Canley)

One of the most eye-catching buildings in Canley is a small public library brightly painted with murals of Elmer the Elephant. There is no graffiti on this building but there are bars at the windows and the front door is heavy and window-less. This library is situated at the end of a long row of shops next to a very green but rather bleak playing field. Most of the shops are hidden behind paint-daubed metal shutters, and only a handful are operating at all. The library itself appears well-stocked with plenty of small chairs for small children and a good selection of large print books for more elderly residents. According to the librarian, this facility is well-used, but unfortunately not everyone uses it to borrow books. Children come in after school because they're bored and want to either talk or do some colouring. Some of the elderly residents use the library as a meeting place, somewhere warm and accessible where they know they will find someone to talk to. Some of the library staff want the facility moved. The presence of older children hanging around makes people feel unsafe, whilst there are too few people passing to ensure that the library serves the larger area well. If the library moves, a valuable meeting place in a poorly-served area will be lost.

Canley is very different from Earlsdon and Hillfields, not least because it lies much further from the city centre. The area feels isolated and rather ignored. Built in the years immediately before and after the Second World War, the housing quality and type adds to this sense of isolation: low-density concrete and steel houses are set back off the road in close-type estates, ensuring that there is no sense of bustle or vibrancy. Some of the housing at the lower end of the area typifies post-war council housing, and here well-kept gardens are interspersed with the litter-strewn grass patches of boarded-up properties. The contrast between the houses which are well looked after, clearly a source of pride, and those which are empty and abandoned, is, like the pressure placed on the library, one of the most obvious signs that this is an area which has been 'slipping'.

Canley as a whole is a large, sprawling area running westwards towards the edge of Coventry. Within Canley itself, residents perceive there to be either two or three separate areas running from east to west: 'There's almost two if not three identities – there's the bottom end of Canley, Prior Deram, the top end and then the bit in the middle.' This demarcation apparently bestows stigma or status upon residents, with the bottom end of Canley being seen as the least desirable part of the area. As a rule, families from either end do not mix.

How has this segmentation come about? Many residents pinned the blame on housing policy. We were told that the 'top end' was built first just before the Second World War and was largely bought by families working for the nearby car plant. The bottom end was built just after the war, and some of the housing was later reserved for council lettings. According to the 1991 census, 56 per cent of the housing in Canley was council-let, and although all Coventry's housing stock has been transferred to housing associations, the figure is unlikely to have changed greatly since then. Long-term residents blame the Council almost entirely for any deterioration of their neighbourhood. They see the problems of the lower end as resulting from more recent housing policies that bring 'difficult' families into the area, and establish a rather transient population. 'You used to get people who stayed in Canley for years, now people move on after 12 to 18 months. They do not get a chance to get interested in the community.' Other concerns relate to anti-social behaviour and a general lack of commitment towards the area.

Despite this fragmentation there is a real sense of identity in Canley, particularly amongst the longer-term residents who seem to feel a close attachment to their homes and their immediate neighbours. They remember when the neighbourhood was a much sought-after location, and are determined that it could achieve that position again:

> We are prepared to put a lot of effort in for no reward because we want everybody to benefit...we don't see ourselves as champions or martyrs. We have lived here a long time and want to get the area up to a standard where people will be saying 'I want to live there'.

There is a strong residents' association and the social focus of older residents is the Canley Social Club in the top end, although use of this Club decreased under previous management and has only recently begun to increase again.

The image of Canley that longer-term residents seem to share is both nostalgic and defensive. They want the area's fortunes to improve but distrust authority. Some people were scathing about the Council, the police, and the local Housing Association. Even the more familiar Co-ordination Team were regarded by some as having failed to live up to their promises. One person complained,

> *I've been at several meetings down there (the old community centre) when bricks have come through the window and you get no response from the police. There is no one you can turn to. If you have one bad neighbour in the area, the Council won't do anything about it.*

There was also a complaint that there was not enough co-ordination or communication between services.

This general suspicion is perhaps understandable given that the area's economic decline was obscured for some time by the focus on ward-level data, but makes it hard for local regeneration services to work effectively in Canley. Many of the people we spoke to were already involved in efforts to turn the neighbourhood around, but we were told both by these individuals and local service providers that many others in Canley are apathetic, cynical and very hard to engage. One man told us 'I'm a member of Neighbourhood Watch, but we can't get it up and running. Nobody is interested.' Another said, 'People are friendly, but they are too scared to commit to anything.' What limited ties there are between residents, then, are inward-looking and very protective. Outsiders are not welcomed, and some said that there would be resistance to any attempts to make the area more mixed. Despite the strong bonds amongst certain families, there seems to be a real deficit of social capital in the area and this makes progress difficult.

There are several factors which make it harder to attain harmonious social relations in a place such as Canley. Even the geography of the area is against this, being spread out over quite a distance, so that it would take twenty to thirty minutes to walk from the bottom end of Canley to the top. There is a bus connection, but services are infrequent, and apparently often cut when there is a shortage of drivers. Some taxi firms are also reluctant to pick up custom in the area.

Another issue concerns the lack of things to do; 'We are the forgotten end of the city with regard to amenities', we were told. There is no natural hub in Canley that might attract people from either end of the locality. Indeed, one person said that the only centre now is Cannon Park – a retail park on the outskirts of the area. Canley also lacks the range of facilities to be found in Earlsdon, or even the number of small shops to be found in Hillfields. The close proximity of Cannon Park with its supermarket and superstores may mean that the area is not a food desert, but the dearth of corner shops or fast food joints means that there is little reason for people to be out on the streets. There is also a significant lack of attractive and open 'congregational spaces'. Canley Social Club now offers good facilities and has a pleasant atmosphere, but because of its location, does not suit everyone. The local pubs are not seen as welcoming due to their bad reputation as places where drugs or stolen goods might be sold, and the community centre and youth club have both effectively shut down.

As well as the shortage of facilities, there is a larger problem with the quality of the public realm in Canley. There may be plenty of open green space, but it consists largely of woodland, wasteland and nature reserves, none of which are as reassuring to use as publicly maintained and well-frequented parks. Similarly, boarded-up shops, litter and graffiti are simply off-putting; this is not a high-quality public environment in which people will feel comfortable lingering or mixing, so people are even less likely to step outside their front doors. The effect of the housing layout and design is to make the neighbourhood feel insecure: with the low-density housing and close-style arrangement, there are too few people around to act as a natural deterrent to crime.

There is a more significant reason why Canley is not experienced as a reassuring neighbourhood. Even if crime levels are relatively normal, the area does suffer from high levels of anti-social behaviour, even by the very young. The damaging activities described ranged from bins being knocked over or set on fire to bricks being thrown though windows. New residents in particular were very critical of this. One said: 'In Dagenham where I moved up from we had more in the way of drugs and burglaries, but we did not have the anti-social behaviour from such young children.' People complained that some kids were 'totally out of control'. They claimed that 'they are just not cared for and the kids know that. Nobody cares where they are or what they are doing.' Others suggested that there was just nothing for the kids to do locally, and even those just hanging around doing no harm tended to be seen as a threat. Many residents said that this behaviour put them off the area, and in particular, made them feel unsafe.

Social relations in Canley are a complex matter. Trust and distrust are to be found in equal measure, with the strongest ties to be found in the most inward-looking groups. Whilst it was not possible for us to understand how this has come about, it was made very clear that the pressures of decline have greatly heightened tensions at a time when co-operation and joint working is most important. The challenge for the local authority and its partners in the area's regeneration is to build up trust, for without this social investment, economic investment may prove futile.

2. Setting out the issues

We all know what an impact the character of community relations can have on local quality of life. For some of our respondents, such as the residents of Earlsdon, a strong sense of community and a vibrant local social life are essential ingredients of the good life. For others, such as many of those living in Canley, the social fragmentation of the area, fear of anti-social behaviour and the general absence of trust make their life significantly tougher. These straightforward observations make it obvious that public policy needs to take account of the impact that proposals and policies have on local social relationships. In this chapter we consider what kinds of tools or interventions policy-makers could apply to help good community relations flourish. This will set up a framework for the discussion on the recommendations emerging from the research in the following chapters.

Why community matters

This report is concerned with the effects of public policy on social relationships at the local or neighbourhood level. Our starting point is the intuition that the quality of community relations matters profoundly to well-being and to many areas of public policy. Although the term 'community' is problematic – it is all to easy to conjure up images of close-knit, homogeneous social cliques (Frazer 1999) – its relevance as a policy concern cannot be denied, at least in so far as it focuses our attention on the importance of *local social ties* (Nash 2002).

Many would argue that in our mobile, electronic, individualistic age, local communities no longer matter. Certainly for some, communities of *identity* and *interest* – friends, work colleagues, clubs, chat-groups on the Internet, campaign organisations – play a larger role than communities of *place*, and many family and friendship networks are fragmented and scattered rather than being very localised around the place we live. In this sense it is true that many of us choose our communities to a far greater extent than we did 100 or even 50 years ago. It is important however, not to over-emphasise this element of choice. At the residential level, those on higher incomes may be able to choose a neighbourhood but they cannot choose their neighbours. Meanwhile, for those less socially or physically mobile, community of place may matter more than any other sort of community, and the character of those relationships must matter all the more precisely because other sources of opportunity and support are not readily available.

Ultimately, it is true for all that the relationships in which we are enmeshed at the neighbourhood level can have a significant impact on the range of opportunities we face and the quality of life we enjoy. We can invest a huge amount in a diffuse community of interest and derive much of our sense of identity from it but we cannot actually live in it. We live in particular places, usually for a length of time that forces us to make some contacts with people who happen to live around us.

What sorts of social ties do people want from their neighbourhood? Most people simply want to feel reassured, not to fear their neighbours, and maybe even trust them to help out on occasion. In this sense, public policy should work to support rather than undermine such a reassuring social environment. IPPR's Communities Initiative was established to help identify ways in which public policy could do more to support this relatively modest but important view of why community counts.

As well as simply making people feel secure and happy, good quality social relations can contribute to our quality of life in various other ways that are highly relevant to policymaking. In the interim publication of IPPR's Communities Initiative three important types of effect were identified (Nash 2002). They are:

- Social capital or 'network effects': whom you know and how well you know them matters.

- 'Socialisation effects': the social environment in which we live or grow up can unconsciously exert pressure on our values, perceptions and expectations.

- 'Attachment effects': when people share a common commitment to their area they are more likely to look after it and to work to ensure its success.

In order to understand how the character of local social relations shapes people's quality of life, and to appreciate fully the policy significance of our observations in Coventry it is worth briefly expanding upon each of these effects.

Ties that bind: how 'community' works

Social capital or network effects

As well as being simply pleasant or unpleasant to engage in, social relationships actually provide us with valuable resources by connecting us to people who can help in certain ways. Friends and family most obviously offer emotional support and comfort, companionship and even financial aid. Although for many people, their closest relationships with friends or extended family are not experienced at the neighbourhood level, relationships with neighbours and other residents can still provide things that we value: services such as baby-sitting, car-washing or gardening; information about, say, job opportunities or good local schools. Sociologists study these 'social networks' (who we are connected to and how) in order to understand whether the range of relationships individuals enjoy gives them all the resources they need. Thus, one sign of healthy community relations might be that residents of an area have access to a wide range of such social resources via a rich and diverse array of local relationships.

Related to the idea of social networks is the concept of 'social capital'. Popularised by theorists such as James Coleman and Robert Putnam, this concept captures the notion that social relationships and the norms that drive them (especially trust) are a valuable collective resource (Coleman 1988; Putnam 1995). High levels of social activity and trust not only ease co-operation and interaction, they are also good for our mental and physical health. Recent research suggests that investment in such relationships by individuals and policy-makers could bring important benefits such as higher educational achievement, improved public health, economic prosperity and more effective local democracy (Putnam 2001). While policy-makers in Britain have often been slow to recognise the importance of maintaining healthy social relations, 'social capital' has now appeared on the policy agenda with the Office of National Statistics (ONS) overseeing a programme of measurement and assessment (ONS 2001), and the Health Development Agency incorporating social capital concerns into its public health research (see for example, Health Education Authority 1999). The Cabinet Office's Performance and Innovation Unit (now the 'Strategy Unit') has also recently published research setting out a possible agenda for maintaining and building social capital (PIU 2002).

Socialisation effects

Although our upbringing and our education are in large part responsible for the norms, values and expectations we develop, it is well accepted that our broader social environment also shapes these. A recent Joseph Rowntree Foundation study noted that our local social networks 'are more than simply routes to opportunities and material resources. The nature and quality of these networks affects how we see ourselves and others, the values we hold and the general quality of lives we lead.' (Forrest and Kearns 1999).

As well as influencing our values and self-understandings, local social networks can also affect our behaviour and levels of achievement via peer-group effects. In social psychology, research has shown that contact with different groups during childhood and early adolescence helps to determine whether or not young people grow up with negatively stereotypical views of members of other social and ethnic groups (Miller and Brewer 1984; Hogg and Abrams 1988). Educational research has shown that whom a child shares a classroom with has a more significant effect on levels of educational achievement than the child's own class background (Mortimore *et al* 1994; Feinstein 1998). All of these socialising effects are likely to be stronger for low-income families who, because of their lower social and geographic mobility are less likely to be exposed to a variety of different social contexts.

This class of effects suggests that the character of local social relations can significantly influence individual welfare by shaping personal development, and consequently encouraging certain expectations, values and behaviour in a way that will limit the range of opportunities available. In this sense, community matters because it helps to determine who we are and how we see our world and to find a place in it that is meaningful for us and others.

Attachment effects

The focus groups carried out in Earlsdon revealed to us that a sense of local identity and attachment to place is something that many people value. This does not mean that residents necessarily want their neighbours to be close friends, or even that they want to know everyone by name. It simply means that some people enjoy knowing that there is a common acknowledgment of their area being 'a decent place to live'. Such a sense of shared identity quite clearly has personal psychological benefit. But just as importantly, it may well help to maintain the quality of the local environment; people who feel an attachment to the place where they live are more likely to look after it, and to ensure that others do the same. As one resident in Earlsdon proudly told us, 'people do like living there so they do look after the environment'.

On the other hand, even slight physical disrepair can make residents feel that no one is looking after their area, and may result in more serious decay or unpleasant behaviour which no one feels any responsibility to prevent. This idea goes some way towards explaining the problems that parts of Canley have experienced. It is also important to note that a shared attachment to place may have very real financial implications. If people do not fly-tip, if they pick up their own litter (and even other people's) then less will have to be spent on street cleaning. The same economies apply to other services ranging from policing to park maintenance.

This description of the various ways in which the character and quality of local social relationships impacts upon individual quality of life and even public spending should make it very clear that policy-makers have good reason to attend to the effects – unintended as well as desired – of policy on community relations. Community matters not just because most people want to live in an area where they feel reassured and comfortable, but also because local relationships can provide important resources, shape our characters and help to maintain the quality of the common environment.

When community breaks down

Discussion so far has emphasised the positive side of community. But it is important to consider a final, more negative reason why public policy needs to pay more attention to its impact on local relationships. That reason is the misery of community breakdown. The riots that took place in Bradford, Burnley and Oldham during the summer of 2001 are extreme examples of what can happen when trust and civility decay and tensions between local groups escalate out of control. Even if only a few people were responsible for the violent behaviour, the tensions that were exposed and the degree of separation between different groups living only streets apart revealed a situation where over-arching community of place had clearly broken down.

Initial inquiries identified numerous factors as contributing to this breakdown in 'social cohesion' and there is good reason to suppose that poverty and unemployment played a significant role. But the effects of specific government policies such as the competitive bidding for regeneration funds, or the lack of suitable youth facilities, were identified as exacerbating the situation. Obviously not all occasions of community decay result in violent behaviour, but the general symptoms (such as anti-social behaviour, social fragmentation, fear and distrust) are unpleasant nonetheless, and this is a very good reason for policy-makers to ensure that where possible they work to support rather than undermine community of place.

What has this got to do with public policy?

Policy-makers get involved when community breaks down violently. But should we not be concerned with the nature of community relations well before such a stage is reached? At first sight it might not be obvious that the health or otherwise of local community relations has much to do with public policy decisions. Whether the residents of a particular area are trusting or suspicious, tolerant or intolerant, engaged or socially apathetic would seem to be in large part a function of individual characters. Earlsdon's social vibrancy might just be a result of its middle-class residents' outlook on life, whilst some of Canley's suspicion could simply result from the harsh realities of living with unemployment and departure of a major employer. Such a view is naïve to the extent that almost every single public decision may ultimately have some effect on the character of local social relations. Housing policy determines who lives next to whom, policies on education, leisure and land use affect who can interact with whom and in what context. Economic policy and regeneration programmes may result in competition arising between social groups in neighbouring areas as the Cantle Report noted last summer (Home Office 2001a). Other policy areas ranging from immigration and citizenship through to welfare and policing will have some impact on local levels of trust and tolerance, and relationships between different groups.

If it would be naïve to believe that public policy had no effect on local social relationships it would be absurd to think that measures to improve them can be devised in isolation from much wider areas of policy. One of the most important elements that makes Canley less reassuring to live in than Earlsdon is the fact that its residents are much poorer, much less likely to be in paid work, and much more vulnerable to the process of alienation and restriction of opportunities summed up as 'social exclusion'. Modest measures to improve the quality of community relations can only do so much: we need them to be accompanied by and integrated with policies to deal with economic polarisation, changing demography and modern work and leisure patterns, discrimination by race, sex and age, regional migration, changing values, educational quality, access to health care, housing quality, and crime and the fear of crime. Our aim is to provide proposals for how 'community-proofing' can be incorporated into policy development in these 'mainstream' areas of debate and provision.

Community is shaped by wider 'structural' factors

Mind the gap: economic polarisation

Despite the growth of the welfare state, the gap between rich and poor has widened considerably over the past forty years. The incomes of the richest 10 per cent rose almost twice as fast (up 140 per cent) between 1961 and 2001 as the incomes of the poorest 10 per cent (up just 72 per cent) (Goodman 2002). This growing polarisation limits the potential for healthy community relations in at least three important aspects. Firstly, those on higher incomes tend to use their resources to separate themselves from those on lower incomes. They move to a better neighbourhood, invest in higher walls and private security, or send the children to a private school. This 'hoarding of privilege' is a major barrier to the advance of social mobility (6 2001) and, at the local level, it means that social networks between higher and lower income groups will be very hard to establish. Physically it means that affluent and struggling areas may exist side-by-side, as in Coventry, with little interaction or overlap between the two.

The polarisation of rich and poor is further problematic when we compare the overall quality of local social ties that each group is likely to enjoy. Although residents in poorer neighbourhoods often experience very strong, supportive social ties with their neighbours, they have little chance to develop the choice- and leisure-based ties that those in more affluent areas experience. Residents in Earlsdon developed their social networks around use of the many neighbourhood amenities or a shared attachment to place, but in Hillfields, residents reported that their local ties grew less from choice, and more from need; namely the need to work together to improve the area. Such ties are also often more inward-looking. This is not an ideal situation, and one which is often exacerbated not just by segregation but by government policy. As Marilyn Taylor notes, there is a misguided tendency to 'prescribe' more local community bonds for those in deprived areas when what they actually need are more social ties that extend *beyond the area* to more affluent groups or people in positions of influence (Taylor 2002). The sense of 'community' experienced by those living in poorer areas is not necessarily a model we would want to promote.

The third sense in which such polarisation can hinder the development of more positive community relations concerns its effects on trust and tolerance. Many policy makers were disappointed with the initial evaluation of mixed tenure housing schemes. Despite their success in terms of avoiding the exclusion and decay associated with mono-tenure sink estates, it was often noted that there was little social interaction between owner-occupiers and social housing tenants (Jupp 1999). In this sense, one might wonder whether it is really too much to ask of people on radically different incomes that they should want to interact. Although areas such as many parts of London which display natural mix of tenures and income groups function very well, the deliberate introduction of people on low incomes into areas occupied mainly by obviously much wealthier people must be carefully handled if it is not to breed resentment or fear and distrust. The change of policy focus in favour of mixed tenure housing is undoubtedly an important advance, but reversing the trend of growing economic polarisation could only help encourage different income groups to mix at the local level.

Demographics: changing people, changing communities

One of the several factors behind the developing housing shortage in the UK (or at least the south-east) is the growth in the number of singleton households. It has been forecast that by 2016 there will be 2.3 million people under the age of 45 living in single-person households, compared to 1.4 million in 1996 (Holmans 2001). The past century has seen a move away from the extended family living together or near to each other, via the classic vision of the nuclear family with its '2.4 children' to a growing acceptance that living alone is fine. Singleton households *per se* need not spell the demise of community, of course; although it is accepted that children are often the catalyst for many local relationships between neighbours, there is little research to show that singles are markedly less sociable than their coupled peers.

Two other demographic changes may have a more significant impact. The 'ageing' of the overall population in some senses bodes well for community ties: more people post-retirement with time on their hands to volunteer, socialise or support local projects. In reality though, older people have so far been under-represented in volunteering (an issue which the Home Office Active Community Unit's *Experience Corps* was established to tackle). Secondly, (although evidence is mixed), longer life may just mean more years of ill health, which with many elderly people living away from their children implies a growing burden of care and potentially greater isolation for the elderly. Finally, the current concerns over pensions and savings mean that unless those in their twenties and thirties start saving considerably more or state pensions rise significantly, we shall eventually see a generation of pensioners potentially too poor to engage in an active and sociable retirement.

The successful integration of women into the workforce potentially poses another demographic challenge to local community. It is often claimed that in the past, women were key community-builders. Willmott and Young's community studies of the 1950s and 1960s revealed a society where women were the community lynchpins who connected up different generations of families, who minded children and offered support to both their men-folk and their friends (Young and Wilmott 1957; 1960). More recently, Barry Wellman has noted that women have traditionally looked after the family's social networks, ensuring that ties with friends and families are maintained even at a distance, and asks whether 'network labour' will come to be shared as domestic labour now increasingly is (Wellman 1999). If correct, these observations imply that as more women 'juggle' the demands of work and families, their contribution to community ties will suffer. It is very hard to assess the truth of this claim, and for various reasons most theorists of the apparent decline of local community and civic spirit, such as Robert Putnam, have avoided making it (Putnam 2001).

Work, rest and play: patterns of employment and leisure

As well as the growing representation of women in the workforce, working patterns in Britain have changed considerably over the past century, with the possible result that many households now have less time for local socialising than in the past. Although working hours have broadly decreased, the number of dual-income families has risen. This effectively means that the total number of hours worked per year in Britain are increasingly concentrated within fewer households (Burkitt 2001). It is also the case that British men work longer hours than employees in most other European countries (an average of 43.6 hours per week compared to the European average of 39.7 (Burkitt 2001)), whilst the growing reliance on e-mail and computers in many professional lines of work, means that work and home are no longer separate domains. The regional imbalance of employment in Britain also means that especially for those in the south-east a significant amount of time is spent just commuting to and from the workplace (Oswald and Benito 1999; DETR 2001a). All of these factors combine to ensure that at least in some households there is little time for getting to know the neighbours.

It has been argued that it is not so much trends in working life that have dented our capacity to engage in local social activity so much as changes in our leisure habits. Putnam, for example, blames what he sees as the demise of American social capital on the rise of television (Putnam 2001). This leisure pursuit, he argues, is an inherently private one, which requires neither the presence of others nor conversation or interaction of any sort. Whilst others have challenged Putnam's argument, the privatisation of leisure should be a real concern. The issue is broader than that of television watching, however; private gyms and indoor leisure facilities have overtaken parks and green spaces as the destination of choice for higher income exercisers, while the impact of computer games on the young is a matter of controversy. More research is needed to determine what effect such changes in our leisure habits exert on patterns of sociability.

Community matters: the policy background

The debates over social capital and community bonds have been of great interest and concern to New Labour in opposition and government. One of the defining features of the Government's approach to policy-making since 1997 is that it has paid homage to the idea of 'community'. This has become a shorthand for the route to many desirable things: a reduction in anti-social behaviour and crime; a 'giving' society of active citizens; better family relationships and fewer broken homes; a more cohesive and tolerant multi-cultural society; and a warm sense of 'well-being' among citizens at the local level. Despite the myriad references to 'community' in Labour's policy statements and speeches, the idea remains hard to pin down. As Melissa Benn says in IPPR's collection of essays on gender politics in the age of New Labour, 'Blairism has had a long and largely abstract romance' with the notion of community (Benn 2001).

Where 'community' has become more concrete as a policy idea is in relation to poverty and urban renewal (so much so, that there is a risk that 'community' becomes a code word for 'the poor in a deprived area'). The area where most attention has been devoted to this concern is regeneration policy, and since 1997 there have been a plethora of reports, documents and initiatives which have made sensible observations as to the importance of social as well as economic investment in deprived neighbourhoods. Thus the New Deal for Communities made a point of establishing local partnerships which would be charged with making decisions as to how the awarded regeneration funding would be spent, (theoretically) building up 'social capital' and facilitating genuinely bottom-up regeneration. In fact, central government has rejected several of the plans put forward by these local partnerships, revealing that it finds it hard to let go. There has been significant under-spend, partly due to the difficulties of getting such partnerships up and running without prior 'capacity-building' (the training and experience that is an essential part of involving local people in the 'turnaround' of their area).

The Social Exclusion Unit, established in 1997, was charged with developing a Neighbourhood Renewal Strategy to ameliorate the pockets of severe deprivation that could be found in relatively small neighbourhoods, and which would help to address not just poverty but the broader range of problems that characterise social exclusion. Policy action teams (PATs) were established to investigate certain key issues such as anti-social behaviour, and neighbourhood management, and these identified policy tools and interventions that could be implemented to help reduce exclusion. Several of these PAT reports noted how particular problems or policy interventions could impact on community relations, and some are referenced in later chapters of this book. The resulting consultation document outlined options for 'reviving communities', where this meant building capacity and supporting healthy local social relations (SEU 2000a). The establishment of the Neighbourhood Renewal Unit and the allocation of new funding means that many of these recommendations are being put into practice, and as well as Neighbourhood Renewal Fund grants themselves, money is also being made available for capacity-building among so-called 'hard-to-reach groups' (Community Empowerment Fund) and for small local projects (Community Chest).

Other areas of government have shown concern for community under a different guise. As noted earlier in this chapter, research into the meaning, causes and effects of 'social capital' has appeared on the agenda of several departmental bodies. Similarly, the riots in several northern English towns last summer meant that issues of 'social cohesion' came to the fore. The two main reports into these disturbances are also helpful in identifying some of the root causes of community breakdown, although the focus on inter-ethnic relations has meant that wider lessons do not seem to have been drawn from these investigations (Home Office 2001a; 2001b). The establishment of the cross-government Community Cohesion Unit does, however, offer some hope that community-supporting policies could yet be given a higher profile within government.

Why isn't this enough?

It might be thought that given the attention already devoted to matters of community, social capital, and now social cohesion, there is no need for a report like this. If all the previous reports and initiatives have correctly captured the dynamics between policy and community then there would appear to be little left to add. But there are several reasons why further comment is needed:

- There has been no mainstream policy response to concerns that policy can damage or fail to support community. The findings of the PAT reports or the Denham and Cantle reports have not been incorporated into mainstream policy-making, but rather have spawned particular recommendations directed only at *the most excluded*.

- There has been too much focus on discrete initiatives, rather than on the whole framework within which policy is formulated. Take the Strategy Unit's social capital report, for example: this aims to identify many policy measures which could build up social capital. But the report fails to consider the effect of much broader policy issues such as the effects of the welfare state on citizens' social networks, or the changing relationship between government and citizen in public service delivery. As the Schools Plus PAT report put it: 'the growing importance of a role for parents as individual consumers has inevitably created tensions with schools' traditional role as servants of a wider community interest' (SEU 2000b).

- There is still insufficient joined-up thinking on this issue. The PAT reports were only required to focus on a very specific policy area, and even the Strategy Unit report reads more like a laundry list than a step-by-step account of how different policy areas interact to support or undermine social capital. Across government, policies that aim to contribute to social capital and underpin community spirit can all too easily be subverted by other policies designed to increase competitiveness and efficiency. Consider for example the revision of planning regulations to make for faster house-building and business development. Will this help build up a sense of 'community' in the areas affected? Or will we get a stream of housing and business developments that lack connections with existing communities or the facilities that make public life possible, such as shops, schools, and transport links?

For all the welcome developments that have flowed from the Government's concern for 'community' in general and for the worst-off neighbourhoods in particular, there is still need for a more methodical approach to the question of how public policy can support community in all areas, whether deprived or affluent, ethnically mixed or homogeneous. The chapters that follow consider each of the three concerns outlined above.

What can public policy do? Tools and interventions

The end of community has been preached ever since the industrial era got underway. Social theorists such as Tönnies and Durkheim predicted that market-based societies would lack traditional patterns of social cohesion, and countless writers since have claimed that 'community' is in decline. As noted above, there certainly are structural factors which make it hard to imagine that most people will ever again live in close-knit, densely interactive social enclaves. But this is no bad thing. If community is to prove a legitimate and viable policy goal, it must not hark back to a more regimented and constricted world of work, religious observation and domestic life that has gone, and that has been abandoned often for good reasons.

As previously noted, the vision of community with which this report is concerned is a 'realist' and minimal one, therefore: it does not imagine that community of place as it was experienced, for good and ill, in previous generations, can be restored. It is, rather, an aspiration to reach a level of civic engagement in the maintenance of local community relations that means people are able to live together in a reassuring social environment, sharing basic respect for the law and each other, enjoying a decent public realm, enjoying a rich mix of social ties, and having the resources for collaborating to maintain and improve the shared environment. It is, however, an important vision, one which if pursued would support and improve quality of life, and would help to avoid the misery of community breakdown. Some of the factors listed in the previous section may make even this vision hard to realise, suggesting for example that we could struggle to achieve such social ties because of pressures at work or changing patterns in leisure. Is there anything then that public policy could do to support healthy local social relations?

The research carried out in Coventry revealed that there are policy tools and interventions that could be employed to support community. Chapters 3 onward will explore these options in greater depth, but it is worth listing the key areas in which policy can make a difference. These recommendations apply to both local and national government, and also, in terms of implementation, have relevance for service deliverers.

Observing the contrast between the three areas studied in Coventry it was immediately clear that some of the differences in the social character of the areas were at least partly due to previous policy decisions. In no case were these decisions likely to have been taken with a view to supporting or undermining community, but this was the result.

The policy areas highlighted as particularly important were:

- Planning and development

- Provision for young people

- Crime reduction and policing

- Design and liveability of the public realm

- Methods of frontline service delivery.

Within these areas there are particular policy tools and interventions which appear to have a significant impact. A list would include:

- Regulation and planning permission

- Master-planning and zoning

- Recruitment and training

- Information delivery and presentation

- Consultation and involvement

- Evaluation and assessment

- Direct provision of services

- Grants and rate levels

To make it clearer how these various policy tools can have an effect on community, each of the next four chapters will capture one important sense in which policy may support or undermine community. The first, Chapter 3, will address the issue of opportunities for interaction. How do policy decisions affect the array of spaces and places at the local level where people can meet? Does policy affect the range of people or social groups likely to interact?

Chapter 4 asks how policy affects the way in which people interact. Specifically, how can policy ensure that neighbourhoods are reassuring places to live and to interact? How can they ensure that trust, tolerance and responsible behaviour thrive?

Chapter 5 looks at the relationship between institutions and community: the way that authority deals with people may affect their relationship with their peers and their opinion of the area itself. This chapter specifically asks how policy can ensure that we come to have trust in governance.

Finally, Chapter 6 considers how policy-makers could be incentivised to think about community. Are there any safeguards that could be put in place to ensure that the impact of decisions on community is always addressed? Given the current culture of evaluation and assessment, can we measure community-building success and reward departments or Councils accordingly?

3. Providing opportunities for interaction

You have a lot of amenities in Earlsdon which means you can almost live there and not go out of Earlsdon. (Long-term resident, Earlsdon)

Quite a few years ago, there used to be a good shopping area here. (Long-term resident, Hillfields)

[When asked where people might meet locally] 'We don't'; 'In houses' (Long-term residents, Canley)

Amenities make community

No policy-maker or local authority can single-handedly 'build community'. National and local government can, however, work to ensure that there are plenty of opportunities for interaction. One of the most noticeable differences between Earlsdon and the other two areas studied was the sheer number of places available for people to meet. The local high street is filled with shops and restaurants, whilst an impressive-looking public library stands opposite a well-used Church and coffee shop, with a small theatre just a couple of streets away. Neither Canley nor Hillfields possess such an extensive range of amenities; there is nowhere to eat lunch in Canley, for instance, apart from the retail park. In Hillfields, one local Church serves as a multi-purpose building: the altar and other features of its services could be moved in order to open up the space fully for non-religious community gatherings.

Earlsdon's wide range of amenities reflects its affluence. But privately-owned shops and restaurants are not the only places to meet there: the Methodist church runs a café and a mother and toddler group, for example, the library is a landmark and meeting point and so on. A few such accessible and affordable public spaces exist in the other communities. A charity-run café opened in Hillfields in 2001 and is gradually building up a significant customer base. Canley boasts an active Social Club, whilst the tiny public library is well-frequented by people of all ages, even if not all go with a view to borrowing books. Clearly it is not just the presence or absence of these sorts of buildings that matters: other factors can have an impact on whether or not facilities such as these will thrive, with local planning and development regulations and transport strategy having a particularly significant effect. Every area, no matter how poor, should and could have some decent spaces and places for interaction; this might mean using existing public facilities such as libraries or health clinics or village halls in a more imaginative manner. The question of how to ensure the provision and best use of those 'congregational' spaces where people can meet is one focus of this chapter.

Some groups within a locality can be particularly ill-served. Our research revealed a common concern in all three areas that there was 'nowhere for young people to go'. Canley, because of its location away from the city centre, presented particular problems, with many local residents reporting that the lack of facilities for teenagers could be one cause of the area's high levels of anti-social behaviour. Recent research by MORI shows that this is by no means an unusual view. In a survey for the Audit Commission, activities for teenagers came out top of people's wish lists for improvements to their area (MORI 2002). A second concern of this chapter is thus how we can ensure that social opportunities are provided for all groups, not just those with the most spending or lobbying power.

As well as affecting the range of opportunities available for interaction, public policy decisions affect who takes up those opportunities. Most discussions of social mix are usually centred around housing tenure and occasionally education. Yet many other policy decisions may affect who can interact with whom in a locality: transport planning, for example, can connect or divide neighbourhoods, leisure policy determines what facilities are available to which groups. These are just two examples of the way in which opportunities for different social groups to interact are affected by policy-makers, often without any deliberate intent. The third concern of this chapter, then is the issue of social mix. How can we ensure that segregation is reduced and different groups are given numerous opportunities to interact casually at the local level?

Planning and development: how to limit community spirit

The three Coventry communities indicate important lessons about planning and development of land. Earlsdon and Hillfields have evolved as 'urban villages' – part of the wider city but with a strong sense of local identity, and in Earlsdon with a capacity for meeting many needs without heading for the city centre. But Hillfields and – to a much greater extent – Canley lack the range of congregational spaces and commercial and community hubs that Earlsdon offers its residents. The social and economic make-up of each community goes a long way to account for the differences between them, but the physical development and planning also matter considerably.

Density and layout

The first and most obvious effect of the planning and development process is its impact on the layout and density of housing. This in turn affects both the character of local social relations, and the sense of community identity. Both Earlsdon and Hillfields enjoy a denser pattern of housing than in Canley, and this contributes to the sense you have in both areas of being in an 'urban village'. The two areas have a bustling vibrancy about them, with the grid-like arrangement of roads ensuring that they are well-used by pedestrians or motorists. In both areas, the density of housing (Georgian terraces and also the tower blocks in Hillfields) ensures that there should be enough people around to support a reasonable array of amenities, although the poor economic status of Hillfields means that few such amenities survive.

Canley offers a stark contrast. Its low-density post-war planned housing estates feel isolated from one another and from the distant city, and also from local shops and other amenities. There are wide green open spaces, but they serve to emphasise the distance between people and amenities rather than enhancing the local environment. Such extremely low-density housing was built in good faith: influenced by the garden-city movement, whereby private space and personal gardens were seen as promoting health and leisure, this suburban sprawl may well have been an easy planning response to the need for quickly-built and cheap post-war housing. In reality, though, by putting a premium on personal space, and the separation of work and residential areas, it is very hard for suburban neighbourhoods to support the range of activities, amenities and services which make a place vibrant (Gwilliam et al 1998; Rogers and Power 2000).

British planning policy already recognises the importance of encouraging higher density developments. Policy and Planning Guidance (PPG) 1 and PPG 3 and the Urban White Paper have all called for greater densities in new housing developments, as well as promotion of mixed use developments following good practice in urban design (DETR, 2000b). It is, however, worth noting that recent housing development in England has been built at 25 homes per hectare on average, while older suburban areas and 'urban villages' here and on the Continent have densities of 35-40 dwellings per hectare, or higher, so there is still some considerable way to go before higher density development has become the norm.

Recommendation

Planning and policy guidance is being redrafted to specify minimum housing density for new urban and suburban development. This approach should be rigorously implemented, with permission only being given for less dense development in special circumstances. Higher density developments should be designed in accordance with leading practice in urban design, sustainable environmental management, and the principles of 'urban village' development.

Congregational spaces

As already noted there were significant differences in the range and quality of 'congregational' spaces to be found in the three neighbourhoods studied. Earlsdon residents benefit from a well-maintained set of old buildings and landmarks which provide ample opportunities for residents to interact, whilst the impressive frontage of the traditional civic spaces helps to define the area's sense of identity. The other two case study areas were less fortunate. Both lack the wide range of shops and restaurants of Earlsdon, and the quality of public spaces is poor. The Hillfields 'village square' is an attempt – still raw and in development – to establish a physical hub for community, but it is as yet, mainly used for parking. Nonetheless, this does at least show that local residents, who requested such a square, (perhaps more than Council planners) are well aware of the importance of public space and places to congregate.

The importance of these issues has recently been recognised by government, although a crosscutting spending review failed to release significant new funding. Many councils, such as Coventry, are developing reasonably sophisticated public realm strategies. There is still room for improvement, however. At the local level, the planning process is still seen as a rather hit and miss affair. One café we visited in Earlsdon occupied the back half of a local art gallery, which fronted on to the high street. Although customers were encouraged to sit in the gallery itself in the chairs provided, café staff could not actually serve drinks there, being instead required to hover in the connecting doorway bearing cappuccinos. The reason for this, we were told, was that planning regulations forbade more than a certain proportion of street frontage to be occupied by restaurants or cafés.

Whilst this particular decision may be perfectly justifiable, it does underline the need for a public realm planning strategy which protects principles of mixed use, but which also recognises the importance of high quality places and spaces for interaction. Earlsdon may not need any more such spaces, but Canley and Hillfields are in dire need, and more action could be taken.

Recommendation

All local authorities (not just those in deprived areas) should conduct a regular audit of 'congregational spaces' in each neighbourhood to determine how much such space is available and what condition it is in. This should cover not just green space or the outdoor public realm but also public facilities such as shops, pubs and community centres. This information could then be used to inform planning decisions, and public spending decisions.

Planning for the future

What all this underlines is the capacity of planning and development policy to foster healthy social relations locally. This has been recognised in debates over the disappointments of the land use planning system, and the vision of a 'new urbanism' that underpins the Government's Urban White Paper and 'Towards an Urban Renaissance', the report of the Urban Task Force, owes a great deal to the ideal of the 'village in the city'. The goal of much urban renewal is to build up 'urban villages' – walkable, environmentally sustainable and attractive, dense, mixed-use development

– in which 'community' will be enhanced and maintained. Unfortunately, research by Cardiff University has shown that the idea of the 'urban village' is given lip service only in many developments, with private developers and public regeneration agencies using the terminology but in practice showing little or no commitment to putting design principles into practice (Biddulph 2002).

This is a matter for some concern, especially given the large-scale developments we can expect to see being built in the south-east in response to the current shortage of homes. The plans for such rapid development of new housing could lead to large-scale sprawl estates such as were seen in the past, with far more attention given to putting up homes than to the infrastructure of schools, community facilities (pubs, churches, children's centres, youth clubs etc) and connections between housing and workplaces and services that do not depend on car use.

Recommendation

The changes in planning regulations that are to be introduced to allow much more house-building need to be accompanied by careful design to avoid the mistakes of past planning and development, and by stringent appraisal of plans against criteria on sustainable development and community relations. It is essential that new privately and publicly funded housing developments do not cast aside widely accepted principles of urban design and liveability in the race to build and fill houses.

Erecting barriers

There is one growing trend which, although not experienced to any great degree in the case study areas, should be a matter of some concern. Social exclusion affects the top of society as well as the bottom, but while we energetically promote 'inclusion' for the worst-off, we are ignoring the growing 'self-exclusion' of the most affluent. The growth in the development of 'gated communities' reflects a retreat by the very affluent behind private security fences and is a very visible statement of lack of confidence and interest in the wider public realm. Such developments are popular because of their association with security and 'exclusiveness', although there is evidence to suggest that they actually make for uncomfortable living, with fear of crime being greater amongst people living in gated communities than amongst those living in non-gated accommodation in the same neighbourhood.

Recommendation

Planning policy should surely be discouraging 'gated' enclave developments, which do nothing to support community and may be promoting a ratchet effect by which more and more people feel that quality of life is best secured by rejecting involvement in the local public realm and seeking a privatised form of security.

The reform of the planning system now in hand thus needs to ensure that sustainable development – full integration of environmental, social and economic goals – is at the heart of future development and land use plans. The forthcoming expansion in housing will be an acid test of how sustainable the new planning and development regime will be for the environment and for community. A key test is the extent to which planning of new developments recognises the need for urban design to help maintain and build community relations.

Recommendation

CABE should monitor and run a built environment version of the Active Community Unit's 'Investor in Community' badge, to be awarded to commercial developers pursuing design policies that fully reflect the principles of sustainable development, namely the integration of economic, social and environmental factors in design and implementation. Public procurement of new homes and other dwellings should exclude developers not achieving this standard.

One major consideration is the scope for community facilities and good design to reduce the incidence and fear of crime and anti-social behaviour, as discussed in Chapter 2. The central issue in this debate at present is the availability of facilities for young people in local communities.

The kids aren't all right: facilities for young people

We're opening up a youth-club here because the kids in Canley have not got anywhere to go...the kids roaming the streets have become a problem. (Long-term resident, Canley)

[We need] somewhere for the kids to stop them causing trouble. (Long-term resident, Canley)

These sentiments are by no means restricted to Coventry: they are a nationwide refrain. They reflect the concern of young people themselves that they have few facilities for leisure and constructive engagement in local life. Polls have shown that although young people between the ages of 16 and 24 are the most frequent users of facilities such as swimming pools, leisure centres and youth or community centres, significant proportions of them are dissatisfied with the services provided (MORI 1998; MORI 2000a).

There is also a mismatch between the sorts of facilities provided for young people and the sorts of places they themselves want to use. In many cases, youth clubs are run from churches or community centres, which can mean they are not dedicated facilities, and that their buildings and facilities are often rather worn-out. A case study undertaken in Surrey by MORI revealed that 44 per cent of local teenagers were unhappy with current provision, and that instead of the normal activities-based format all they really wanted was somewhere permanent to 'hang out' with friends. Their ideal provision was 'a youth centre like on Byker Grove' with space for relaxing, some sort of sports facilities and management that retained some 'street cred' (MORI 2000b).

The quotations above also reflect the frequent complaints from adults that young people 'hanging around' are a nuisance or even a threat. Some Coventry residents said that their perception of young people as threatening and as a source of anti-social behaviour was significant enough to stop them walking around their neighbourhood or using certain routes. One elderly woman recounted how local children would kick a football against the side of her house. It might not do any actual damage, but the activity made her feel insecure and she no longer spent so much time doing chores or chatting outside her home. The perception of young people as a disruptive and negative element of local life thus plays a strong part in many citizens' views on the decline of local quality of life and the 'liveability' of public space.

This raises important questions about the role of facilities for young people in community-building, about the relationships that are developed between children, teenagers and adults in neighbourhoods, and about the adequacy of existing services available to support young people. In other words, the argument is that decent amenities for young people are essential not only to support that group, but also to ensure that the effectiveness of the local public realm as a space for diverse and rich public interaction is not undermined.

The problem of 'hanging around': policies on youth facilities

These concerns have not gone unnoticed in policy circles. The Policy Action Team 12 report, produced as a backdrop to the National Strategy for Neighbourhood Renewal, explicitly mentioned these issues:

> In all the PAT's visits and discussions with young people, the lack of safe, interesting and affordable leisure facilities emerged as a huge issue. A strong theme was that young people were criticised for hanging around, or amusing themselves in disruptive ways, when there were no high-quality alternatives on offer. Where good facilities do exist, cost, location and transport were cited as severe obstacles to participation.

That report went on to note:

> A worrying feature of many poor neighbourhoods is the extent to which young people are seen as a 'problem'. In some areas this clearly has its roots in genuinely high levels of anti-social behaviour by children and

teenagers...In other areas a loss of confidence in young people may be without real justification and can act against community cohesion. (SEU 2000c).

The problem of inadequate provision is also recognised by the general public. In the recent surveys carried out for the Audit Commission on local quality of life, 43 per cent of all respondents claimed that in their area, activities for teenagers most needed improving, this response topping the study in both rural and urban localities. Reductions in crime levels, which was the second-most popular response, received the assent of just 29 per cent of those interviewed (MORI 2002).

What all this implies is that some of the most corrosive problems for local community spirit, namely fear of crime and anti-social behaviour, and poor relations between teenagers and adults, could be significantly affected by *relatively modest action to improve local facilities for the young*. Given that the message seems so clear, we might expect current policy to reflect these priorities. It is certainly fair to say that there has been significant development in policy provision for young people under the Blair government, not least with the establishment of a Children and Young People's Unit (CYPU) designed to improve key public services for this group in response to the findings of PAT 12 (SEU 2000c).

Despite this, the focus has so far not extended to the provision of facilities for young people, with most of the newest plans targeting social exclusion and education. Thus we have seen the establishment of the Connexions service, a £420 million initiative designed to co-ordinate the key organisations working with young people aged 13-19, as well as providing personal and careers guidance for young people themselves. The Youth Service is also to be revitalised to bring it into line with the requirements of the Connexions framework. Some of the smaller initiatives introduced by the CYPU will have the result of supporting activities and local amenities for young people. The Spaces for Sport and Art initiative is awarding £130 million to local authorities to enable them to improve arts and sports facilities in the 65 most deprived areas in England, whilst £50 million has been set aside by the National Lottery New Opportunities Fund to pay for summer activities and outdoor adventure for the most disengaged. Both these initiatives are admirable. But what is lacking is any mainstream response to the problem of inadequate local amenities for the young.

The trouble with youth facilities

There are three main reasons why provision of spaces and amenities for children and teenagers is often inadequate. The first is a factor of the budgeting process. Local authorities receive a proportion of their education funding for support of the local Youth Service. Traditionally, this money has been used both to maintain facilities such as youth clubs, as well as to pay for the services of youth workers. Meanwhile, most councils' budgets for leisure are spent on maintaining indoor facilities, arts and tourist attractions rather than parks and green spaces or the more flexible, informal spaces that suit youth activities such as skate-boarding. As noted in the Final Report of the Urban Green Spaces Task Force, the pattern of local authority leisure spending has changed significantly over the past twenty years. Spending on urban parks and open spaces has decreased from 43 per cent of local authority leisure services expenditure in 1976/77, to only 31 per cent in 1998/99 (DTLR 2002). Outdoor sport and recreation receive the same proportion as they did twenty years ago – just 3 per cent – while, the report suggests, a greater share of the funding has gone to arts, theatres and museums and tourist features. In most cases there has also been a real failure to bring young people themselves into decision-making about what sorts of amenities are needed.

The second reason concerns the focus of the Youth Service itself. As an education-based service answerable to OFSTED, there has unsurprisingly been little scope for a purely leisure-based approach. This is not to deny the importance of youth work, or indeed to under-estimate the extent to which even leisure-based activities can be educational in the broadest sense. Given their remit, it is understandable why youth service resources have rarely made the provision and maintenance of spaces and amenities a priority.

This is even more understandable in the light of the financial pressure faced by local Youth Services. Funding for the Youth Service is not ring-fenced, and as councils have faced real cuts in their education budgets, one easy option has been to cut back spending on the Youth Service. As the Department for Education and Skills (DfES) has recorded, there is huge variation in the spending allocated by local authorities, ranging from £261 per 13-19 year-old (in Kensington and Chelsea) to just £30 per head in Hampshire and Portsmouth. Median local authority spend is £59 per head, and only 11 authorities spent more than two per cent of overall education spending on youth services in 1999-2000 (DfES 2001).

Despite these barriers there is room for improvement within the existing policy framework. The youth work system could be compatible with an approach that focuses more on provision of facilities. The National Youth Agency (NYA) has recently proposed a framework for an improved Youth Service. As part of that structure they proposed a Youth Pledge of Entitlement which could help to shape local service delivery and to hold local decision-makers to account. Although this would have to be agreed locally, one key element of the suggested pledge is that young people should have access to 'a safe, warm, well-equipped meeting place within a bus ride, with facilities for drama, music, sport, voluntary action and international experience' (NYA 2001). That framework would also positively recommend more involvement for young people in decisions about such amenities.

The Pledge also suggested that young people should have access to 'a youth-led "youth audit" project, involving young people in auditing and evaluating the services available to them locally' (NYA 2001).

Taking action on youth issues

If progress is to be made in ensuring that all young people have access to decent local facilities where they can meet with friends and enjoy activities in such a way that their presence in public spaces is not seen as threatening, then it is essential that the following measures are undertaken:

- There must be more co-ordination between Council leisure services and Council youth services.

- Children and teenagers must be more systematically involved in processes of decision-making.

- More leisure spending must be diverted to informal rather than formal or site-based facilities.

Specifically, three policy proposals should be considered in order to ensure that lack of facilities for young people does not threaten local social cohesion. The first concerns a best practice model of partnership working; the second a range of localised leisure services which should be prioritised; and the third suggests a revitalised model of youth clubs to which all young people could have access.

Somerset County Council is just one example of an authority where a very successful partnership has been established bringing together youth workers, leisure development officers, community development workers and parks/open spaces officers. This group was then able to devise a strategy for developing appropriate leisure facilities for young people, with an emphasis on facilities that were very accessible and largely free at the point of use.

Recommendation

This model of leisure & youth-work partnership working would fit well within the Connexions framework and should be adopted as widely as possible to ensure that best use is made of limited financial resources, and in particular so that the needs of young people for access to decent leisure facilities can shore up rather than undermine local community development and cohesion. Were this model to be more widely adopted it would be essential that such networks at the very least consult local children and teenagers, but more appropriately there should be a provision for young people to be included in the youth leisure network itself.

It is essential that some of the new initiatives adopted by the CYPU are mainstreamed and that funding is diverted towards the provision of informal sports and leisure-based facilities for children in all areas not just in the most deprived wards.

Recommendation

Local authority leisure services should ensure that they offer a range of amenities specifically for young people. The main principle underlying this provision is that those facilities should be highly localised, easily accessible and free at the point of access. Spaces provided should be as flexible and informal as possible to ensure their suitability for a variety of pursuits such as skateboarding, BMX, climbing, and kick-about.

There is good evidence, as noted above, that across the country there is a strong feeling that teenagers lack sufficient provision for leisure outside the home and that this contributes to problems of anti-social behaviour and the fear felt by residents for groups of young people 'hanging around'. The Government's new Community Cohesion Unit, based in the Home Office, has undertaken a 'health check' on summertime activities for young people in districts felt to be at risk of trouble. Summer activity schemes for young people – covering the age range 11-25 – are intended to help avoid the disturbances that damaged community relations in places such as Oldham and Bradford. There is a separate scheme under the Connexions umbrella, for 13-19 year-olds in areas suffering from high levels of crime and truancy. Some £25 million is being spent on these various programmes. How effective they are is unclear as yet. The Youth Justice Board has claimed that the 'Splash' scheme for leisure activities in high-crime areas has helped reduce levels of offending but Home Office researchers have concluded that initial schemes in 2000 did not produce any appreciable effects (Gaber 2002; Loxley *et al* 2002).

But these schemes, however desirable, are *temporary* responses – in the case of Splash, hastily set up and lacking in consultation with the intended users of the facilities, according to Loxley *et al* (2002) – to deep-seated problems. Although Connexions offers a promising framework within which to join up services for young people, large-scale capital investment is beyond its current remit. If we take seriously the evidence that the absence of decent facilities – ranging from youth clubs to up-to-date sports centres – does indeed raise the risk of anti-social behaviour, crime and other community-eroding activity, then something more ambitious is called for.

Our proposal is that in all the areas eligible for Neighbourhood Renewal funding there should be a programme of development of facilities for young people which would rejuvenate the youth club concept. The national name for this programme could be 'Young Clubs' (not only reflecting the target group but also in tribute to the great social scientist and innovator Lord Michael Young, who died in 2001 and who made a huge contribution to the study and development of 'community' in the UK). The Young Club programme would not impose a uniform model of provision. Rather, it would be a process of collaborative design, development and management between young people and their community bodies. In each area, funding would be made available for young people and community bodies to undertake an assessment of what is needed, and to design solutions. Facilities, once developed, would be managed in part by local young people, and linked to schools and colleges and also to other community amenities. If this approach proved viable, the Young Club initiative could be extended beyond the Neighbourhood Renewal Fund areas.

The benefits of this kind of initiative could be: meeting widely expressed demand for better (or any) facilities for youth; involving young people in decision-making and 'ownership' of their services; bringing young people into constructive contact with the wider community; and – the test of such a venture – much reduced incidence of crime and unpleasant behaviour among teenagers. It would differ from and add value to existing provision by Connexions, which focuses on education and work, by bringing the issue of leisure facilities to the fore; and it would provide a long-term strategic framework within which programmes such as Splash could move beyond temporary projects for bored youth in the summertime. The Young Club initiative would be a focus for joining up Connexions work with leisure issues, and both with the new citizenship education element of the national curriculum, introduced in September 2002.

Recommendation

A programme of capital investment for the development or construction of 'Young Clubs' should be introduced in all areas eligible for Neighbourhood Renewal funding, and possibly extended at a later date. Young people should be involved in the design, development and management of these facilities.

Melting-pots and mosaics: the question of social mix

It's always been a melting-pot since the sixties. It makes a very colourful area. (New resident, Hillfields)

The council in their infinite wisdom thought we have got a few problem families, we'll put them in this nice area and it'll rub off on them. But what happened was when they moved in, the nicer people started to move out. (Long-term resident, Canley)

I think that minorities are driven out of this area...nobody wants them here. (New resident, Canley)

Public policy can create or destroy opportunities for interaction not just by determining which facilities are provided where, but also by affecting which groups do or do not have access to those spaces. If we are concerned that local social relationships should be reassuring and familiar, it is important that all social groups are comfortable interacting with each other. This need not mean that rich and poor neighbours have to know and like each other, or that different cultural groups should undertake the same social pursuits. 'Community cohesion' cannot and should not mean full integration of groups who have long been apart and feel they have little in common. While melting-pots sound desirable, the reality is that groups tend to form 'mosaics', and the challenge to policy and to local communities themselves is to ensure that the mosaic makes a diverse yet harmonious picture, rather than simply being an expression of fragmentation.

We contend that 'cohesion' should be taken to mean that all social groups should feel able to enjoy an area's public life free from fear of attack, abuse or hostility, and that the area should not be riven by forced segregation in any form. People may not wish to have much to do with one another beyond being civil, law-abiding and tolerant but they should feel able to interact in public and feel reassured that the public realm is safe for them. That which is unfamiliar can very soon become a source of fear, while, as experiences in Bradford, Burnley and Oldham have shown, inter-group tensions can mount where sections of the population live lives that run in parallel but never touch. More positively, the benefits to be won from social networks means that, at least on grounds of equal opportunity, public policy should actively support the development of a rich and diverse range of social ties at the local level. In this context, policy should support not just those local amenities which provide opportunities for interaction, but should also ensure that those facilities provide genuine opportunities for different local social groups to mix.

Housing and diversity

With England's history of Garden Cities and Quaker-built estates such as Bourneville, mixed tenure has long been accepted as a way of ensuring that neighbourhoods are economically and socially sustainable. In recent years, mixed tenure in housing has become the most common method of promoting social mix. The 2000 Housing Green Paper (DETR 2000a) enshrined this principle as the key means of avoiding further marginalisation of social housing and its occupants. The rationale for this policy change was primarily economic, the intention being to ensure that social housing should no longer be concentrated on single estates where universally low incomes reduce the area's economic viability and encourage low ambition and anti-social activities.

Despite this, many social commentators have hoped that tenure mix might also have more favourable social outcomes, via the creation of new social networks between residents of different tenure types. That this has not been observed, at least amongst first-generation residents, has consequently been seen by some as a significant failure of the mixed tenure model (Jupp 1999; Atkinson and Kintrea 1998). The most positive results seem to emerge from 'pepper-potting', or the mixing of different tenure types within a single street, but unfortunately this model is less likely to be employed by developers and housing associations because of the higher costs of managing such a scheme.

Recommendation

Housing associations and property developers could be offered financial and other incentives by the Treasury for 'pepper-potting' social housing to reflect the higher design and management costs of this strategy.

In fact it could be much too early to tell whether social links could yet be forged through mixed tenure schemes. There are encouraging signs from research looking at the interaction habits of second-generation mixed tenure residents that over time, more crosscutting social networks may arise. Further to this, the development of new communication technologies such as e-mail and intranets may smooth the process of interaction at the local level. Although experiments have yet to be undertaken in Britain, Canadian trials have shown that local e-mail networks can help to build connections between residents who might not otherwise interact (Hampton and Wellman 2000). The particular value of these findings comes in their apparently positive message that far from replacing face-to-face communication, local computer-mediated communication (CMC) can actually help to encourage more personal contact. In the Canadian trials such CMC also proved effective in building links between residents of different ethnic groups, although due to the lack of tenure mix no conclusions could be drawn on the technology's potential to link different income groups. It would be very interesting to see whether computer-mediated communication in such 'wired-up communities' has the potential to build up more connections between more affluent residents and their social housing neighbours, an opportunity missed by recent DFES pilots to bring information and communication technologies (ICTs) to low-income households.

Recommendation

More research is needed into the potential of CMCs to promote interaction between residents of different social groups. To aid this process, and to support social integration, government-supported developments such as Millennium Villages could incorporate easy-to-use computer-mediated communication such as neighbourhood e-mail networks and intranets.

Although these are positive signs, the focus on integration at the residential level could still be misplaced. Mixed tenure is ultimately desirable to ensure the economic viability of estates and to help avoid further stigmatisation of the social housing sector. But it may be too much to expect of people that such mixing should lead to the creation and maintenance of social ties across class and other divisions. People who live next to each other do not have to interact and it may even be hard to get different groups to live next to each other in the first place. Perhaps we should look for other ways of encouraging more interaction between different groups at the local level.

Schools and social mix

The most obvious candidate here is education. Research has shown, after all, that social stereotypes can most effectively be challenged by routine meeting and co-operative activity when young. Situations where children have to work together in teams are amongst the most important opportunities for challenging such stereotypes (Sherif *et al* 1961; Aronson *et al* 1978). Bearing this in mind, the introduction of comprehensive education in the 1960s should seem a particularly positive move. However, quite apart from the continuing existence of a separate and parallel private education tier which enables more affluent families to hoard educational privilege, two policies pursued by the Labour government could reduce opportunities for interaction between local children from different social groups.

First, the Government's continued support for the principle of parental choice in education means that local families are no longer guaranteed to meet fellow residents through the ties their children create. Children may be sent to schools outside the area if this seems to offer superior educational opportunities. It has been suggested that this undermines one important means of ensuring that all local families, whatever their income, ethnicity or politics have some common ties (Worpole 2000a).

In reality, this claim may be exaggerated, and whilst few attempts have been made to collate statistics which would enable us to judge how this policy has affected the likelihood that children will attend their local school, anecdotal reports for particular Local Education Authorities suggests it may be mistaken. It is true that the average length of the journey to school for secondary age children increased from 2.3 to 3.3 miles (45 per cent) over the period 1985/86 to 1997/99 and for primary school children, from 1.1 to 1.5 miles (DETR 2001b), but this is at least partly explained by the amalgamation of some local schools. Other studies have looked not at the mix of children from different localities in any one school, but rather the mix of children from different income groups. In those studies, it has been argued that the effect of parental choice on school admissions are less important than the impact of local education authority allocations strategies and economic trends (for example, Gorard 2000; Noden 2001). More research on this issue is clearly needed if we are to determine whether the market-based principle of parental choice will indeed lessen the likelihood that local children from different social groups will mix at school.

The second educational policy which has implications for local social integration is the extended state funding of faith schools. Whilst Catholic and Anglican schools have long been supported by public funds, non-Christian schools are far less likely to benefit from such support. According to the statistics released by the Department for Education and Employment in 2000, state support was then provided for 4716 Church of England schools, 2108 Catholic schools, 30 Jewish schools and one Sikh school (DfEE 2000). The recent education Green Paper offers a commitment to increase the number of state-funded religious schools, including Muslim, Sikh or Orthodox Jewish schools (DfES 2001). The Church of England aims to open a further 100 secondary schools.

This approach is clearly to be recommended on grounds of consistency and also equality of opportunity in so far as it recognises that Britain is now a multi-cultural society and that state funding should not be disproportionately used to subsidise Christian schools over non-Christian schools. But it is less than clear that any state funding of faith-based schools is supportive of integration and social cohesion. As the admittedly partisan British Humanist society has noted

> if children grow up within a circumscribed culture, if their friends and peers are mostly from the same religion and hence also, very likely, the same ethnic group, and if they rarely meet or learn to live with others from different backgrounds, this is hardly calculated to promote the acceptance and recognition of diversity (Humanist Philosophers' Group 2001).

Unfortunately this matter is highly complex. The pupil intake in secular schools can be homogenous and that that of faith-based schools can be heterogeneous. Many faith-based schools reserve a number of places for children from the local catchment area. There may even be good community-supporting arguments for the continued state funding of faith schools, if for example, it can be shown that by developing confidence or a set of values which can underpin citizenship, pupils of such schools are likely to contribute to the health of their local community relationships. The Denham report into the disturbances in Bradford, Burnley and Oldham does recognise the complexities of this issue, and writes about the problem not of faith schools, but of 'mono-cultural' schools, and proposes accordingly that all schools should endeavour to limit their intake from one culture or ethnicity (Home Office 2001b). In other words, the expansion of state funding for faith schools may not necessarily be detrimental to goals of social mix, but it does impose a greater responsibility on government and schools to ensure that other ways of integrating pupils be promoted.

In the light of this, a new development linking the four main faiths in Britain could be very significant and worthy of encouragement by Government. The Church of England is backing a plan for a new multi-faith secondary school in the London borough of Westminster, to take in Christian, Muslim, Hindu and Jewish children. The pupils will learn, eat and play together and find out about each other's faiths; and while some religious observances will be separate, there will be multi-faith assemblies. It is planned that this should be the first of similar initiatives around the country. Such ventures deserve close scrutiny for the lessons they offer on more flexible ways of meeting the demand for faith-based education at the same time as the desire for more community cohesion and less segregation by ethnicity and religion.

Recommendation

As suggested by the Denham report, partnerships should be formed between local schools of different social profiles to ensure opportunities for children to interact outside their cultural, ethnic or income group are provided. These partnerships should provide a basis for joint sports and arts activities, for joint citizenship education programmes, and project or curriculum-based links.

Streets as meeting places

What other mechanisms are there for encouraging social mix and community cohesion? Perhaps the key is to focus on the situations in which people will voluntarily mingle and interact. Sports, leisure, entertainment and cinema, eating, drinking and shopping: all of these are things we naturally enjoy and may not mind so much with whom we do them. Some of these activities will expose us to the presence of other, different people; some will demand more and require that we interact and co-operate with those others. A healthy public realm and the potential for building rich and diverse local social networks require both. Without the everyday mundane encounters of passing people in the street, queuing together in shops, talking to the man who runs the post-office, it is impossible to imagine how any level of generalised trust can arise. These are the sorts of encounters which may ultimately leave people as strangers, but familiar strangers nonetheless. As Jane Jacobs put it:

> The sum of such casual, public contact at a local level – most of it fortuitous, most of it associated with errands, all of it metred by the person concerned and not thrust upon him by anyone – is a feeling for the public identity of people, a web of public respect and trust, and a resource in time of personal or neighbourhood need. The absence of this trust is a disaster to a city street. Its cultivation cannot be institutionalised. And above all, *it implies no private commitments.* (Jacobs 1961 italics in original).

Cultural amenities and community-building

Joint activities such as sports, arts and drama on the other hand may well create private commitments, and as such are ways of building stronger relationships and ties between individuals of different groups. Knocking a football around, taking part in a play or producing community artwork are very good ways of getting to know other people in a neutral environment. It is thus particularly important that there are facilities for these activities to take place outside schools in such a way that young people from all backgrounds can participate together. The recently published Draft Guidance on Community Cohesion issued by the Local Government Association emphasises the importance of expanding leisure and cultural activities for young people and suggests mainstreaming summer activities to run year round, as well as organising inter-school events (LGA 2002). This might help to prevent the development of the sort of social relationships which a recent ESRC study described as 'tectonic' (Robson and Butler 2001). Observing the social networks of residents in Brixton these researchers noted that whilst people actively applauded the diversity and vibrancy of the area, there was little interaction between the incoming white middle classes and other ethnic and income groups, and even less trust.

Recommendation

The Community Fund, NOF, Sports England and the Arts Council should co-ordinate work on developing new programmes of funding specifically for leisure, sports and arts projects which support diversity and the integration of different social groups. Sport England could also run an ambassadorship scheme helping local teams and key sporting figures to champion local projects which support diversity and integration (such as the successful Football Unites, Racism Divides scheme).

As well as suggesting that a wide range of local leisure amenities and opportunities should be available, these arguments also imply that the location of such facilities may prove to be important. Some services such as shops and pubs may obviously belong in the centre of a locality, providing it with a natural heart in a way that shores up local identity and offers residents an obvious place to meet. Other services such as sports or leisure centres, cinemas or theatres may not need to be so central, and could be better placed on the edge of a locality to naturally draw in different types of people from surrounding areas.

This point is worth emphasising. There is a tendency in some of the regeneration literature to see neighbourhoods as 'enclaves': self-contained, inward-looking areas which should hold all the key facilities that local residents need but which give them little reason to travel elsewhere. Little attention is given to ways of attracting people in from the outside, even if that would provide a valuable social and economic resource. Once we recognise the importance of social mix, and the value of different types of people mingling and interacting, the appeal of a different model becomes apparent. Elizabeth Frazer recommends the alternative 'overlapping intermingling localities' model, whereby social amenities on the edge of neighbourhoods come to be used by residents of other areas in a way that ensures diversity and mixing of groups (Frazer 1999). The location of facilities such as schools, sports grounds and leisure centres on such boundaries may be particularly important in helping to bridge the gap between neighbouring poor and wealthy areas.

The potential impact of this effect was illustrated by the experience of one area studied in Coventry. The Canley area currently has two primary schools, one located at either end. Most parents send their child to the school nearer them, an action which some suggested contributes to the area's social fragmentation, and the stigmatisation of the lower end. Plans for a new school in the centre of the neighbourhood to replace both existing facilities have been met with opposition, but some residents argued that the move might at least help to unify the area over the next generation by ensuring that children from all over Canley can mix and integrate within a single school.

Another strategy might be to support the development of speciality services in a locality. Just as the long-running hardware store in Hillfields attracts residents from all over Coventry, so Earlsdon's organic shop reported a range of clients coming from several areas in the city. Both of these approaches are successful means of attracting in new and perhaps different groups of people.

Recommendation

Local authorities could voluntarily undertake (perhaps as part of the development of a social cohesion strategy where this applies) a social mix study. This would identify the degree of mixing in key areas: at the residential level, in schools, and public spaces or leisure services, possibly by using footfall or other consumer information. It would enable policy-makers to determine which amenities are most successful at bringing different groups together, as well as highlighting situations where different social groups never mingle at all. This information should then be incorporated into local retail strategies, public realm strategies, and planning and development decisions in order to ensure that across the area as a whole social mix is supported and that the 'enclave' model of community is avoided.

4. Reassuring neighbourhoods

It is a poor area; some poor areas have a hostile feel to them. Here there is an acceptance of the difficulties of the area, and there is a nice atmosphere. It is a very difficult atmosphere to define...it's like a perfume or a drink, you have the components of a bad atmosphere, but the product is quite different. (New resident, Hillfields)

People just tend to look reasonably happy...probably because they can walk to the shops and feel safe. (New resident, Earlsdon)

There is a lot of fear around, a lot of it is unnecessary. Something needs to be done. (New resident, Canley)

In search of a decent place to live

The previous chapter looked at ways in which public policy could help to support community by protecting and providing opportunities for interaction between residents. The presumption was that although policy-makers cannot intervene directly to make people trust each other or to become friends, they *can* do a great deal to promote a framework within which this is possible. One essential component of that framework is clearly a lively and vibrant public realm with many spaces and places for different groups to pass through and mix. But as the Coventry residents made quite plain, it is not enough to provide opportunities for interaction. The public realm must feel safe enough for residents to be happy using it. Unless the neighbourhood feels reassuring, no amount of new facilities will encourage people to leave the privacy of their own homes and cars to mingle with strangers and acquaintances alike.

There are three key policy factors which affect how reassuring a neighbourhood feels. One concerns the design and 'liveability' of the area, the latter now a potent phrase in policymaking circles, as the quality of local environments is recognised more fully as a factor in social exclusion and inclusion. Related to the question of liveability is the issue of car use and traffic patterns, which affect local quality of life in ways that go far beyond problems of noise or pollution. The third key factor is the way in which crime and anti-social behaviour are dealt with by the authorities. All of these have long been recognised to have a significant impact on local quality of life, yet, as the evidence gathered in Coventry reveals, public policy is still failing to handle these issues in a consistent and appropriate manner.

Liveability: how clean is our alley?

Too many dumped cars, broken bottles everywhere. (Long-term resident, Hillfields)

Canley is very lucky because we have so much green-belt around us. (Long-term residents, Canley)

The concept of liveability is simple. It captures the idea that our quality of life is dramatically affected by the quality, appearance and use of the public spaces we dwell amongst. It covers issues such as 'the quality of the streetscape, whether it is clean, safe and easily walkable, or litter-strewn, graffitied and carved-up by rat-runs or trunk-roads' (Worpole 2001). Although many of these issues have long been part of the urban renewal agenda, the recognition of liveability as an over-arching policy theme marks an important step. Tony Blair highlighted the Government's concern for liveability in a major speech on quality of life in 2001 (Blair 2001), yet the recent dedicated cross-cutting spending review has failed to release any new sums of public money, just as the report of the Urban Green Spaces Task Force only succeeded in releasing £500 million over five years (DTLR 2002).

The quality of the public realm can have an enormous impact on local social relations. Just as heavy traffic will reduce the social use people make of streets and neighbourhoods, so graffiti, litter, decay and vandalism will discourage residents from using public space. Although most of the residents we spoke to in Hillfields were generally positive about the area, the most heartfelt complaints concerned the quality of the local environment. Dumped cars, bottles and litter dropped by clubbers and students, condoms and needles left by prostitutes and their clients: these may only be a problem in some parts of Hillfields, but for residents in those streets they create a general reluctance to step outside the front door. The boarded-up shops, vandalised toilets and graffitied shutters in the lower end of Canley create a similar feeling of menace. The effect of such detritus is to encourage the feeling that no one is looking after the area, and consequently, no one is looking after your safety. Sometimes described as the 'broken window syndrome' it has also been observed that even such cosmetic damage can invite more serious anti-social or even criminal behaviour (Wilson and Kelling 1982).

The issue of liveability concerns not just grey concrete spaces such as streets and pavements, but also the quality of urban and rural green spaces. The contrast between the neighbourhoods we studied was remarkable on this issue. Hillfields lacks almost any green space, to the extent that one early-years teacher we spoke to worried that some local children never got to play out of doors. Canley, on the other hand, enjoys plenty of wild green space, a feature which many residents highlighted as central to their attachment to the area, although the scrubland, woods and nature reserve differ markedly from Earlsdon's manicured parks.

Although few of the streets that we visited in the three areas seemed to be especially 'unliveable' there was a significant contrast between the environmental quality of streets in Earlsdon and those of the poorer neighbourhoods. This underlines the extent to which environmental poverty is still a source of injustice, and explains why further action on improving the liveability of our public realm is essential.

Principles for 'liveability': what makes a community reassuring?

There is no graffiti on the shop doorways, hardly any shops have shutters. (Long-term resident, Earlsdon)

The dynamics of the streets by the way they are designed helps to bring people together, like the village square. Architecture helps to shape people. (New resident, Hillfields)

One of the problems with Canley is that because it is geographically strung out, it hasn't got a centre. (Long-term resident, Canley)

First impressions of an area count for a lot, and walking around the three areas studied in Coventry produced very different experiences. Earlsdon's leafy green streets and smart terraces were instantly reassuring, making one feel that residents might look after you, the stranger, as they would their properties and streets. The grid-shaped road system, bustling high street and friendly corner shops ensure that there is plenty of movement, and consequently, plenty of opportunities for any criminal or anti-social activity to be observed.

In many ways, Hillfields offers a similar experience. Although there is a sharp contrast between the rows of terraced Georgian red-brick and the dominating concrete tower blocks, in daylight this area feels similarly reassuring. The proliferation of local schools guarantees that almost everywhere there are signs of children and family life. The problems with prostitution and drug-dealing, though, mean that, by night, there is perhaps more reason to be wary. However this is not so much a result of the way the area is designed or maintained but rather the appropriate perception of risk in the face of known criminal activity which could take place anywhere.

Canley, by contrast, can feel less welcoming and in places, even intimidating. Its suburban and largely close-based character means that it feels like a dead-end rather than a space which many people will pass through, and the houses are often set back some distance from the road. There are few people to be seen, and at times the main signs of human habitation come in the form of litter-strewn grass verges alternating with well cared-for gardens.

That the physical character of these neighbourhoods should affect our perceptions of risk and security is perfectly reasonable. Jane Jacobs classically analysed the factors that make such a difference. Her three principles for 'a city equipped to handle strangers' perfectly capture the key physical features that make an urban space feel reassuring:

- Public and private space must be clearly demarcated so that it is clear which is which.

- There must be 'eyes on the street': shops and businesses must directly face on to the street.

- Streets and pavements must have enough passers-by to increase the number of 'eyes on the street' and to give those in adjacent buildings something to look out on (Jacobs 1961).

To these three principles, Jacobs adds a fourth that echoes the argument of the previous chapter:

> The basic requisite for such surveillance is a substantial quantity of stores and other public places sprinkled along the sidewalks of a district.

One further factor could be added, as an extension of Jacob's third principle: the presence of figures of authority in public places to deter bad behaviour and reassure citizens. One persistent theme in research on public space in recent years has been the withdrawal from the streetscape of figures such as police on the beat, park keepers or rangers, caretakers in tower blocks and schools, with the result that many residents complain that the police have become invisible to the community, and that the decline of our public parks has been accelerated (Worpole 1998). In many walks around our Coventry neighbourhoods, sightings of police constables, park keepers and wardens were extremely rare.

We contend that the best way to make sense of the idea of 'liveability' is to draw on these insights from Jacobs. Her focus is on the reassurance offered by an area to its residents and to strangers: how far can people feel at ease in the place? Together these four principles offer a suitable starting point for the design of reassuring and therefore community-friendly neighbourhoods. Notably they contradict the current assumption that the best or only way to protect space is to offer defensive surveillance either in the form of CCTV or private security.

What is currently being done?

There is a wide range of measures currently in place to deal with standards of environmental quality and design, but none of them go far enough and there is certainly still a need for a more integrated approach to 'liveability' across policy areas – planning, housing, policing, transport and so on. On the issue of design, the establishment of the non-departmental public body CABE (Commission for Architecture and the Built Environment) is an extremely positive move. One of the first tasks undertaken by CABE was to produce and publish a set of urban design principles, with the acknowledgement that 'Good design can help create lively places with distinctive character; streets and public spaces that are safe, accessible, pleasant to use and human in scale; and places that inspire because of the imagination and sensitivity of their designers' (CABE 2000). These principles comprise the guidance that accompanies PPG 1.

The streetscape

On the issue of the quality of the street, a variety of measures have been introduced ranging from the introduction of neighbourhood and street wardens with powers to levy on the spot fines for people littering or spoiling the public realm; to funding available through the Community Fund and New Opportunities Fund for improvements in urban green spaces. The American-style Business Improvement Districts which are currently being piloted are expected to encourage new private sector investment in enhancement of the public realm, although this is unlikely to help in areas which are facing economic decline.

But the scale of the task of improving urban design and maintenance is underlined by CABE in a report drawing on 12 case studies around the UK on maintenance of the 'streetscape' (CABE, 2002a): this research concluded that the mass of available advice on good urban design for local environments was being neglected by local authorities, with the result that many streets in the UK are 'alienating and unappealing non-places'. Problems of maintenance and neglect of good design practice, says CABE, reflect 'inherent barriers in the institutional, regulatory and management frameworks'. A MORI survey for the Audit Commission showed that when people are asked to think about what most needs improving in their area, road and pavement repairs, street cleaning and traffic congestion are seen as more pressing issues than health services, housing and education (MORI 2002). Surveys carried out for CABE also revealed that over half the people polled would be prepared to pay an extra £20 per year in Council Tax in order to improve the appearance of their local area (CABE 2002b). In particular, the neglect of maintenance has been a major factor in the decline of our open spaces, especially of parks, and this reflects inadequate provision in budgets over decades for maintenance of infrastructure.

Green spaces

The decay of many of Britain's urban parks and green spaces has finally been recognised with the publication of the recent report of the Urban Green Spaces Taskforce. Undermined by budget cuts, reduced maintenance and the loss of dedicated wardens or keepers, these spaces are very much in need of a revival. Although the recent report has proved helpful in highlighting the scale of the problem, the sum of money allocated for the restoration and maintenance of urban green spaces is very low. The further problem of fragmented responsibilities is likely to prove even harder to address. As Ken Worpole noted in an article on liveability, this fragmentation has reached extraordinary levels when up to fourteen agencies might be responsible for the upkeep of a single cemetery (Worpole 2001).

Recommendation

The recommendations of the Task Force on Urban Green Spaces (DTLR, 2002) should be taken up, to increase substantially public spending on parks and other urban green spaces, improve coordination between agencies at local level, develop better management systems, improve the exchange of ideas and lessons between areas, and establish a better base of information and indicators on provision. All capital projects involving the creation or redesign of public spaces should include a long-term maintenance plan, securing sufficient funds for maintenance work and staffing.

As the experience of Hillfields residents shows, there is also a need in many places for the creation of new green spaces. Neither inner-city or suburban areas should lack high quality, accessible green space, and developers could be encouraged to provide this. There is also a need to ensure that existing open spaces for leisure and sport – such as playing fields – are not lost, and that more use can be made of them by the whole community. The revision of Planning Guidance 17 (PPG 17) on spaces for sport and leisure is welcome in this regard, as it promises to halt the loss of playing fields to development and places great emphasis on the provision of high-quality open spaces for sport and leisure and the contribution these can make to quality of life and community relations (ODPM 2002a). But the guidance needs to be implemented well at the local level and 'joined up' effectively with initiatives on maintenance and improvement of green spaces, parks and the streetscape.

Recommendation

The current principle of 'planning gain' should be used more systematically to encourage the creation and high-quality maintenance of new high-quality public green spaces in towns and cities. The revised Planning Guidance 17 (PPG17) on open spaces for leisure and sports should be rigorously applied by local authorities, and integrated with new local strategies on parks, streets and green spaces.

Crime and design

Despite the fact that 75 per cent of the crime prevention budget between 1996 and 1998 was spent on installing CCTV, a recent survey has shown that CCTV is more effective at reducing the fear of crime than crime itself (Armitage 2002). This suggests that there is certainly room to explore more positive approaches to making neighbourhoods more reassuring. This should be possible as the connection between good design and security has certainly been recognised. The 'Secured By Design' initiative run by the Association of Chief Police Officers (ACPO) aims to reduce incidents of crime by designing for a more secure environment. Unfortunately, like the money poured into closed circuit surveillance, this method tends to adopt a defensive view of space in direct contradiction to Jacobs' more positive principles which promote use and re-population rather than physical methods of keeping 'undesirables' out.

Recommendation

More crime prevention money should be directed towards positive rather than defensive strategies so that initiatives targeting say design or lighting in the public realm could actively encourage more use of public space. CABE should work with local authorities, NACRO and the Home Office to research and develop such a strategy.

Mainstreaming

The main concern about present initiatives is that they represent a very piecemeal response to the problem and do nothing to address larger issues around the long-term reductions in spending on maintenance of the public realm, and the fragmentation of responsibility that has accompanied this. The 'mainstreaming' suggestion of the Urban Task Force, namely that local authorities should draw up a 'public realm strategy' has not so far been adopted but this could make a significant difference (Urban Task Force 1999). The other notable omission is anything resembling a long-term strategy to improve the quality of the public realm. Only by adopting strategies which look decades ahead have cities such as Copenhagen managed to reverse traffic expansion and also dramatically improve the liveability of neighbourhoods. The reforms of the planning system announced in July 2002 (ODPM 2002) point to new attempts to join up policies better through the land use planning process, aimed at integrating social, environmental and economic factors. There is to be a new system of Local Development Frameworks, which will provide the 'map' for local land use planning. It is vital that these changes are well integrated with Community Strategies drawn up by local authorities as the overarching strategic plans for their areas, and with neighbourhood renewal programmes and the work of Local Strategic Partnerships: otherwise the scope for fragmentation and confusion, already great at the local level in relation to plans and frameworks, will be increased.

Recommendation

Local authorities are charged with drawing up Community Strategies on long-term well-being for their areas. The process should include the creation, based on genuine consultation with residents, of 'public realm strategies' as recommended by the Urban Task Force, with plans looking up to twenty years ahead. As part of this strategy a comprehensive 'public space audit' should be undertaken of existing congregational spaces and their quality as recommended in the previous chapter, with this information being used to inform planning and development. In particular, the quality of public space – the streetscape, parks, green spaces – should be focused upon by Local Strategic Partnerships set up to oversee the process of Neighbourhood Renewal in disadvantaged localities. These processes should be linked effectively to the new Local Development Frameworks on land use planning.

There is a mass of good research and many examples of leading practice in 'joined-up' approaches to urban design for 'sustainable communities' (Barton 2000). These are projects where economic development, environmental quality and social cohesion are not treated as separate issues but seen as inter-connected and treated as such in the process of decision-making. The problem is really just that existing policy-making and funding practices make it hard to ensure that 'best practice' is applied and that 'joining-up' actually happens to useful effect. In theory the new processes at local level for 'community planning' – producing long-term strategies for community well-being – offer much greater scope for this to happen. In practice we need to reinforce efforts to break down barriers to more joined-up action, which has been sadly lacking on issues such as public space.

Traffic and community

> *Because it is a fairly poor area, less people own cars, they are on foot, walking past people and talking to them.* (New resident, Hillfields)

How *reassuring* a neighbourhood feels is more than just a matter of housing density and style; factors such as traffic levels can also have a negative effect. It is accepted that traffic patterns can affect our quality of life by creating pollution and noise, but their impact on social relations is often ignored. Public policy in Britain has certainly been slow to face up to this issue. Whereas many other European countries and cities have consciously adopted strategies to control car use and restore pedestrian priority, Britain lags behind. Oxford is the only city in Britain to have reversed traffic growth in the last 15 years, whilst cars in London travel at the same speed on average as did horse-drawn carriages at the end of the 19th century (Rogers and Power 2000).

Car use and traffic patterns exert three important effects on local social relations. All of these were demonstrated in the areas we studied. The first way that traffic undermines community is captured well by the quotation given above. If you are in a car, you are in a private rather than a public space, and as such, you need not interact with anyone. Residents in Hillfields felt that this was one reason why people got to know or at least recognise their neighbours; the relatively low incomes in the area plus its proximity to the city centre meant that levels of car ownership were lower than normal, ensuring that people would more often meet on the streets.

The second effect of car use on community is related to the first, and concerns not whom pedestrians will meet but the facilities they will use. Hillfields is admittedly a much higher-density neighbourhood than Canley, nonetheless it does support an impressive range of corner shops, Halal butchers and video stores. Despite its proximity to the city centre these amenities survive, at least partly because they are easily accessible on foot.

The third way in which car use shapes local social relations has been documented in studies in San Francisco, and more recently in other European cities. In the 1970s, Don Appleyard and Mark Lintell demonstrated that there is an inverse correlation between levels of contact between neighbours and traffic density (Appleyard *et al* 1981). The more traffic there is, the fewer occasions on which people undertake activities outside their houses, and the lower the number of friends and acquaintances developed in that neighbourhood. The effects of this trend can be observed in Canley where a very busy arterial road effectively bisects two estates.

It is worth noting that not all traffic is bad. As one Council officer told us, Canley has actually suffered because there are no roads that run through the estates to other areas. If there were, he surmised, local shops might have gained enough business from passing trade to stay open. But the environmental effects of high levels of traffic, and its role in deterring pedestrians and residents from using the street are significant problems for community relations. Moreover, the intensity of car use removes people from the streetscape and may play a part in making crime and anti-social activity less visible.

Despite the strength of the car lobby, British policy-makers are beginning to accept the weight of these arguments and one of the most promising developments has been the recent expansion of the Home Zone scheme. This government scheme, initially piloted in just nine areas, involves the re-designing of a street so that it meets the interests of pedestrians and cyclists rather than motorists. Long used on the continent, Home Zones involve a more radical re-think than simply putting in sleeping policemen. An extra £30 million was released last year to allow the creation of more Home Zones, and there are signs that local authorities are initiating their own projects. PPG 3 was revised in 2000 to require that local planning authorities should 'focus on the quality of the places and living environments being created and give priority to the needs of pedestrians rather than the movement and parking of vehicles (DETR 2000b). The main hurdles to further expansion of Home Zones are the ultimate responsibility of local highways authorities for this issue, and the loud voice of local car users and the national car lobby. Further research is also needed into the potential as an improvement to Home Zones offered by more integrated transport strategies such as are now being trailed on the continent.

Recommendation

The domination of the streetscape by traffic is a major factor in the erosion of local social links and quality of life in communities. Local authorities should make the planning and implementation of Home Zones and 20mph zones a priority.

Crime and anti-social behaviour

I walk around here, morning, noon and night. It's safer now than it was ten years ago. There's more cameras around. (Long-term resident, Hillfields)

[of a certain street] It's well-known for being a no-go area. (New resident, Canley)

There is a lot of nuisance style behaviour, one of the latest things is knocking the dustbins over. What do they achieve? (New resident, Canley)

That crime and anti-social behaviour undermine healthy community relations is not news, least of all to people on the receiving end. But it has taken a long time for policymakers to get the message, and comprehensive analysis and policy development have only taken place on the issues in recent years. Since 1997, several of Labour's anti-crime initiatives have focused on reducing the fear of crime as well as crime itself, although recent figures suggest that the public are becoming more not less nervous, with perceived levels of crime rising whilst recorded incidences drop or remain largely static (Simmons *et al* 2002). Measures to deal with antisocial behaviour such as Anti-Social Behaviour Orders (ASBOs) were introduced in the wake of findings by a Policy Action Team set up by the Social Exclusion Unit, and the recent Police Reform White Paper addresses calls for more policemen on the beat by proposing methods for reducing paper-work and introducing a new 'civilian' patrol (Home Office 2001b). Given that there is so much policy focus on making neighbourhoods more reassuring by dealing with crime and anti-social behaviour, do we need to make further comment? We do if existing policy is less than fully effective.

The impact that crime and anti-social behaviour exert on people's patterns of sociability is all too obvious in Coventry. Two of the areas studied experienced problems: Hillfields with prostitution and drug-dealing; Canley with unpleasant and irresponsible behaviour, often by very young children, and a newer problem of drug-dealing. In both cases, residents that we spoke to expressed negative feelings about the impact on their quality of life. All three of the effects identified by the Policy Action Team were observed: some residents feared going out, especially at night, others said they would move on from the areas as soon as they could, whilst many felt the stigmatising effects of being associated with a supposedly 'high-crime' area (SEU 2000d).

What was resoundingly clear from all the discussions we held in these neighbourhoods was the apparent intractability of the problems. Prostitution has long been an issue in Hillfields, and there is not much confidence that matters are improving. Many of the people we spoke to resented this problem not because it necessarily made them feel unsafe, but because they felt it projected a negative image of the area which made *outsiders* feel unsafe, and so perpetuated the stigmatisation of Hillfields. Canley residents, on the other hand, who experience relatively less crime felt that the high levels of anti-social behaviour did make people's lives miserable on a daily basis. In that neighbourhood, the problem has become compounded by the fact that even a few incidents of bad behaviour have been sufficient for some, such as the elderly, to feel threatened by young people even when no harm is being done. More frequent and obvious policing was generally seen as the answer, but at the same time it was not clear that residents placed any real trust in police officers. What more can be done to reduce such crime and anti-social behaviour?

Crime and the community: coping with deep-rooted troubles

Problems such as those experienced in Hillfields affect local residents' quality of life in two ways. First, the presence of prostitutes on the streets at night means that other female residents risk being approached by kerb-crawlers, and creates an atmosphere of insecurity which would make many think twice about walking around after dark. Second, the high level of domestic burglary (74.9 incidents/1000 population in 1999/00) required to feed the drug habits of those attracted to the area by the presence of dealers means that people may not even feel safe in their own homes (Coventry City Council 2001). It is a testament to the strength of community spirit that most of the people we spoke to in Hillfields felt that these were localised problems caused by people from outside the area, and did not let these problems affect their attachment to their neighbourhood. As the area's recent 'community visioning' process revealed though, people do very much want these issues to be dealt with (WATCH 2002).

The question of how to deal with the problem of prostitution is complex. Speaking to both the police, residents and community groups, it seems clear that the usual methods of imposing fines or ASBOs simply do not work. Fines encourage prostitutes to take on more clients in order to repay them, whilst ASBOs are complicated and time-consuming to impose and may only result in the problem moving a short distance away. There appeared to be a surprising degree of consensus on all sides that the best answer would be to legalise and regulate brothels, whilst clamping down hard on kerb-crawlers. This would enable police and other authorities to monitor and control prostitution in the area and would make residents feel far more secure.

Such a strategy would be highly controversial and would require further investigation and consultation before we could recommend it as supporting community. The point to be drawn from this issue is that on some seemingly insoluble problems there may be a tension between what is required to make a neighbourhood reassuring by eradicating some of the fear of crime, and that which would be required to get rid of the crime itself. Visible control and oversight of problems such as prostitution or even drug-taking can reassure residents more effectively than simply treating the practice as an offence. If the government is serious about tackling the fear of crime, this may require a dramatic reassessment of the status of certain 'crimes' and strategies for dealing with them.

Performance measurement and targets: the inefficiency of efficiency measures

There can be no doubt that recent policing reforms have increased central control of the forces, indeed the current Police White Paper extends this principle by proposing the introduction of a national Standards Unit and a right of intervention for the Home Secretary in removing the Chief Officers of under-performing forces (Home Office 2001b). While a degree of such centralisation may be necessary to ensure consistency in training and methods, it is not clear that the introduction of nationally set performance indicators goes any way at all towards helping police to react to local problems and build up trust with residents. In particular, the existence of the 130 or so key performance indicators and the nationally set policing priorities make it very hard to reassure residents that resources are being targeted at the most important local problems. As one Chief Constable has put it,

> National objectives, the National Crime Reduction Strategy and the myriad of Best Value performance indicators have crowded out local objectives to the extent that local consultation forums are often dominated by police managers explaining what they cannot do because of the constraints of the national agenda. (Neyroud 2001)

The second way in which nationally set standards can undermine effective community policing concerns the repeated complaint by police officers that national auditors cannot measure what they do. This is not a churlish refusal to accept appropriate evaluation and assessment processes, but rather a realistic concern that the essence of good policing cannot be captured by the chosen quantitative performance indicators. While it may be easy to record and measure stop and search incidents, crime reports or arrests, it is far harder to record and compare how relationships are built up with local residents, or problems solved by mediation and discussion before they result in criminal acts. Good community policing and crime prevention are simply not recognised and rewarded by present performance indicators, and as such, indicator-driven policing will reduce the likelihood that these are accorded the importance they deserve. Efficiency targets do not assist community-building.

Recommendation

The scale of Key Performance Indicators and national objectives for policing should be reassessed in the light of arguments given above. Alternatives should be considered, including assessment according to local objectives set by forces themselves in conjunction with Crime and Disorder Reduction Partnerships and significant involvement of local residents. Where possible representative local residents should be involved in the oversight of police activity as suggested by the Chief Constable of Thames Valley Police (Neyroud 2001).

Joined-up thinking is not working

Effective community policing requires close working with other relevant authorities such as housing associations, social services, the education authority, the probation service and the health authority. While recent initiatives such as 'Safer Estates' have helped to institutionalise these partnerships, there is still a vacuum of responsibility, with confusion over which body should take the lead for any particular problem.

Dealing with anti-social behaviour very often requires the co-operation of several services, one of the reasons why it is so hard to do successfully. Contact may be needed with housing associations to identify and warn trouble-makers, with schools to deal with truancy, police to deliver anti-social behaviour orders and probation services or social services to follow up. Police interviewed in Coventry spoke of the frustration of working with housing associations to produce ASBOs and then finding that the required support is not provided by other local services. Concerns were also raised that anti-social behaviour might not best be treated as a 'crime'. Other more positive interventions to change the behaviour of the individual concerned could be more fruitful, especially where children or young people are involved. It would be particularly interesting to see whether the procedures currently practiced in restorative justice (discussed below) have anything to offer in this situation.

Fewer than 500 ASBOs have been delivered since their introduction in 1999, largely because of their complexity and the length of the process. David Blunkett, in 2002, announced the introduction of 'interim anti-social behaviour orders' which would enable an order to be made at a preliminary court appearance pending a full hearing. This could speed up the process, but does little to address the difficulties of the partnership working required for effective control of anti-social behaviour, or the larger concerns about the effects of treating anti-social behaviour as a crime.

Recommendation

More research is needed to help us identify effective methods of preventing or dealing with anti-social behaviour, looking at the effects of the wider policy framework as well as strategies which might avoid recourse to the courts.

Policing and community: career structures and training

The importance of community policing was recognised in the recent Police Reform White Paper when it was suggested that extra pay should be available for officers at the 'sharp end of public service'. All the officers we spoke to felt that this was important as community and beat policing is currently very poorly regarded within the force. They reported that this encouraged many beat officers to seek promotion as quickly as possible, undermining local trust and meaning that experience and local knowledge cannot be capitalised upon. One of the reasons why many residents we spoke to in Hillfields were largely positive about the police was because all could name a particular local PC who had worked in the area for many years. His visibility, trustworthiness and local understanding helped people to feel that any problems arising would be dealt with effectively.

Whilst there is thus a need to encourage continuity of service for community police, more could be done to ensure that local knowledge and experience is passed on through the training process. New beat officers should be introduced to key local figures as a matter of course, but it appears that this does not always happen. Police officers also need to be taught how to talk and engage more empathically with different people in order for effective relationship-building to take place.

One approach to dealing with these concerns could be to make more use of courses such as those run by the charity Common Purpose, which bring together people from different services and sectors in cities to expose them to each other's priorities, problems and ideas. Common Purpose courses involve visits to key services (prisons, hospitals, schools etc) and a programme of building up awareness of the scope for 'joining up' across policy areas, sectors and services. This model could be used more extensively to improve linkages between service providers.

> **Recommendation**
>
> Common Purpose-type training courses should be run within each local authority several times a year. All individuals starting work on the front-line of the various public authorities should be required to undertake a course as part of their training. This would provide a way of developing understanding about local issues, help to identify key local figures and would build personal links between members of the relevant authorities.

The White Paper has suggested that a new tier of police could be introduced called the civilian 'Community Support Officer' (Home Office 2001b). Although this could prove helpful if it results in more 'eyes on the street', there are other reasons why this might be a weak idea, not least in so far as it diverts scarce financial resources away from recruiting new police officers. Firstly, it communicates the message that police are too busy to have a real local presence, which could further undermine residents' trust. Secondly, where there are significant anti-social behaviour problems, as in Canley, it will be very difficult for even a uniformed community member to deal with those problems authoritatively. Residents in Hillfields already have a neighbourhood warden, and although they were largely positive about this, they felt he was only useful in providing some extra 'eyes and ears on the street'. He was seen as generally powerless, a sentiment which was echoed by Canley residents who very vocally rejected the idea of a warden.

> **Recommendation**
>
> Career and pay structures should be reassessed and restructured by the Police Negotiation Board to ensure that community policing is valued more fully within the force.

Restorative justice

As well as raising some of the issues which make it difficult for police to work effectively, it is worth highlighting one new crime reduction method which has achieved surprising success. Restorative justice is a new perspective on criminal justice whereby an offender can be brought together with victims, and/or the wider community to accept responsibility for the offence. Although so far seen as experimental and in need of further development, one force (Thames Valley Police) has transformed its cautioning process to include the restorative element, and several others have trialed the idea. Early results show that the process of bringing an offender face-to-face with the injured party/ parties has helped both victims and offenders to come to terms with the impact of the crime, and in a significant number of cases, the process appears to reduce the risk of re-offending (Hoyle and Young 2002; Miers *et al* 2001). It appears to be a particularly successful method for dealing with young and first-time offenders.

Although research so far has been dedicated to the use of restorative justice as a response to petty crimes such as theft, criminal damage or handling of stolen goods, there is potential for this strategy to be used in response to episodes of anti-social behaviour, especially if support could be gained from other relevant agencies such as Registered Social Landlords or Social Services.

Recommendation

More police forces to explore the potential of restorative justice, and to consult with the community on the possible value of trialing this as a strategy for dealing with anti-social behaviour, especially that committed by young people.

---

5. Building trust in governance

WATCH is succeeding by bringing the community together and helping people organise themselves (member of the WATCH team, Hillfields)

We need professionals to 'marry into' the area! (community worker and resident, Canley)

I don't think the authorities should promise to do things and then not bother. (Long-term resident, Canley)

The previous two chapters have identified ways in which public policy might provide a supportive framework within which community could thrive. The focus on providing opportunities for interaction and a reassuring environment for that interaction says little about the type of community relations that we would hope this to promote, but a key ingredient of healthy community relationships is *trust*. If we want to support community then we need to do more than just provide opportunities for people to interact, we need to try, where possible, to help foster trust.

Trust is valuable in at least two different contexts. First, 'inter-personal trust' is required in order for people to co-operate with one another, and perhaps even more importantly, it is needed in order for people to feel comfortable and reassured in the place where they live. Design and effective policing may well help people to feel secure, but unless they trust their neighbours some degree of fear will remain. The second type of relationship in which trust matters concerns not individuals relating to their neighbours or friends, but to institutions. 'Institutional trust' is required to oil the interaction between individuals and institutions; manifested in how residents might feel about their service providers or political representatives.

Each of these elements needs to be healthy before we can speak of positive and supportive community relations. Places or groups where internal bonds are strong and trusting but external relations are weak and lacking in trust, are essentially enclaves, with a defensive view of the world. Places where internal and external bonds are weak and untrusting are highly vulnerable to a spiral of decline, as is feared by many in Canley. Places that have vibrant internal relations and are seen as desirable areas to live may yet have poor links to public agencies and lack of trust in local governance, and also may see themselves as having little common cause with worse-off places. And finally, local public agencies that are not much trusted by communities are hampered in making any positive contribution to the well-being of neighbourhoods and in engaging citizens in the local process of democratic governance.

Front-line service delivery

They need to live in the area and understand a bit more about the community, what needs changing. (New resident, Hillfields)

[on WATCH] 'A lot of people who work here have a genuine passion for the area and the people.' (New resident, Hillfields)

They [the Council] would have to come out and meet you and come into the area more, make themselves more well-known. (Long-term residents, Earsldon)

Each of the three areas studied displayed quite different patterns of trust and distrust. In terms of inter-personal trust, levels of trust were much as we would have expected given the different character of each area. Residents in Earlsdon said that they felt quite comfortable with one another and loyal to the neighbourhood, although some residents feared going out at night. In Canley, much greater pressure is placed on people's willingness to trust in strangers and neighbours alike. The prevalence of crime, anti-social behaviour and fear of crime erodes trust between residents, notably between older people and local children or teenagers, who are widely perceived as threatening. In Hillfields, the economic problems of the area over decades and the transience of a significant part of the population – with many students, refugees and other passers-through – could have led to a similar situation of low trust as we find in Canley. However, here the existence of a strong network of community-led initiatives seems to have played a vital role in preventing such developments.

Questions about *institutional* trust threw up rather more unexpected answers. In Earlsdon, the economic self-reliance of the community, the richness of facilities and the general affluence of the culture mean that there is little contact with public agencies beyond the use of routine services (such as waste collection, policing, schools). Perhaps as a result of this, Earlsdon respondents tended to feel more trust in local residents and businesses than they did in local public service agents and the Council in general, and indeed, many were quite scathing about the latter despite the high quality of their public environment. For Hillfields and Canley, the relative deprivation of the areas makes for a much greater sense of relationship with the Council and public agencies, though not necessarily a trusting one. In fact there turned out to be a significant disparity between the two areas' relationship with authority.

In Canley the sense of alienation from public agencies was palpable. We were repeatedly told that people had no confidence in the capacity or interest of the Council in listening to them, or in the Area Co-ordination Team to deliver real improvements. Housing providers came in for similar criticism, although admittedly, Hillfields residents saved their most critical comments for this agency too. More generally though, the Hillfields residents we spoke to had a fairly positive attitude both about the capacity of the Council and Area Co-ordination to look after their interests and about their own ability to communicate any concerns to the relevant agencies. One common criticism that we encountered in both Hillfields and Canley, however, concerned the lack of understanding of local issues shown by professionals and the degree to which public agencies have little local presence.

Understanding the lay of the land

The different experience of the three areas raised interesting points about how public agencies could do more to foster a better relationship with citizens. The most significant issue in all three neighbourhoods concerned the extent to which contact and the circumstances of contact affect trust. Earlsdon residents unsurprisingly have the least contact with public agencies, and despite the fact that Coventry City Council obviously works hard to maintain the quality of the parks, streets and services in the area, few people said that they would trust the Council to look after the area's best interests. In Canley and Hillfields the problem is not lack of contact but the circumstances of contact. Frequent contact, it would seem, need not breed familiarity and trust. Instead, front-line service deliverers such as police, council officers or housing providers can be seen as distant and lacking any real connection to the area, which makes it harder for residents to trust their judgement.

In both cases the distance of professionals from the 'front-lines' was cited repeatedly as a barrier to the development of trust; a sentiment which might be summarised as 'why should we trust someone who has no real understanding of how we live?' In many areas where public policy aims to 'build community' the lack of resident professionals is obvious. Often it is only members of the Church of England and other denominations and religions who actually live in the deprived neighbourhoods. Councillors, police, housing professionals and others live anywhere but the areas of greatest need. There are striking exceptions – Bob Holman, the community development campaigner in the Easterhouse area of Glasgow, and the Secretary of State for Work and Pensions, Andrew Smith, in Blackbird Leys estate in Oxford – but they are all too rare. It did seem true in Coventry that few public agents now reside in the localities they serve. Most of the council officers we spoke to in Coventry City Council lived in Earlsdon, Kenilworth or Leamington. Police and teachers also tended to live outside their area of work.

There are, of course, plenty of good reasons why such a trend might develop: people avoid living in the areas that demand the most policy attention for reasons of security, to put a distance between work and home, and to live in reassuring and pleasant places rather than rough and demanding ones. In the south-east, many public servants have simply been priced out of the areas they work in, unable to afford to rent or buy in the over-heated property market. In other areas, schemes which previously offered subsidised housing to, say, police or nurses have now been stopped, partly because of cost but also because they were recognised to leave individuals open to attack or harassment.

Despite these good reasons, such separation is not healthy for community-building and for trust. People living in hard-hit areas need to feel that the public servants they deal with fully understand their problems, just as much as local residents need to understand the broader policy issues affecting them. Such understanding on the part of service providers requires some capacity to empathise with the person concerned, to imagine what it must be like to live that sort of life. Unfortunately, it seems that this empathy will no longer be developed naturally as a result of living in the locality concerned, and at present it forms no part of public servants' training. At the very least, 'capacity-building' for community development and regeneration must be a two-way process; and for professionals it must mean much greater exposure to the places they are charged with regenerating and maintaining in partnership with local people. One approach to the issue is to encourage much more regular contact between service providers and local communities up to actual periods of residence in neighbourhoods of greatest need. Such contact could be linked to wider training programmes, such as Common Purpose courses for linking policy-makers across sectors and services.

Recommendation

Extensive 'capacity-building' training should be given to all new MPs, councillors and members of LSPs, involving regular visits to local areas and in particular to the worst-off ones, and frequent contact with residents' groups. Frontline service deliverers such as teachers, police and housing officers dealing with particular areas should also undergo an induction process which familiarises them with the place, with key local figures and an understanding of local issues. Training for MPs and members of major local partnerships should involve periods of residence in the most deprived neighbourhoods – say of 3-4 weeks – as a means of overcoming perceptions of remoteness, lack of knowledge of issue, and 'empathy gaps' between professionals and residents of deprived areas. These approaches could be linked to Common Purpose courses (see also Chapter 4) bringing together professionals from different sectors and services.

Recommendation

More effort should be made to foster, train and recruit frontline service staff from the localities in which services operate, for example, in housing and employment services. Incentives and support should be available to encourage others to move to the area they serve.

Dealing with people

Local knowledge and understanding is clearly important to help build a relationship between frontline service deliverers and citizens, but skills and experience also make a difference. One organisation which attracted our attention on this account was a not-for-profit regeneration company, managed by local residents in Hillfields. WATCH (Working Actively To Change Hillfields) was established in 1998 as the outcome of a partnership set up between the Council and local residents. The company describes itself as independent and autonomous, and emphasises that it is accountable only to local residents. Its objective is apparently 'to seek to secure, co-ordinate and manage resources for the social, economic and environmental improvement of the area for the benefit of people living and working in Hillfields' (WATCH 1998).

Although the company operates several different services, including community development and an impressive new ICT centre for training and community use, it was the employment services which caught our attention. Their employment and advice centre attracts up to 400 clients a week, and many of these are from excluded or hard-to-reach groups. The centre has now replaced the previous statutory provision. Unemployment in the area has proved stubborn to deal with, partly due to the absence of any major employers, but despite this, the centre has an increasingly impressive success rate in finding employment for its clients. Residents we spoke to who had used the service said that a key feature of its success was the type of people employed to give advice. Although advisors were not necessarily Hillfields residents, there was a feeling that many of them had experienced unemployment in the past or understood the sort of hurdles that faced the clients. As well as displaying a valuable degree of empathy, these advisors were felt to offer a very flexible service, helping their clients to fill out forms, to find out about benefits or even to arrange childcare. This flexibility apparently helps to build trust perhaps by making clients feel that they are receiving a genuinely personalised service, that they are respected and taken seriously, and are more than just a number. Our respondents spoke very highly of the quality of this service, and indeed of the activities of WATCH more generally.

Recommendation

More effort should be made to recruit and train individuals who have direct experience of unemployment, housing difficulties and so on. The flexibility and personalisation of service offered by programmes such as the New Deal should be made available as part of mainstream employment services, with the possibility of extending the model of provision to other services such as housing.

Recommendation

There should be long-term support for community-led umbrella agencies such as WATCH, rather than the current system of pump-priming and funding for 'new' initiatives which makes it hard for these organisations to retain good staff due to the constant financial uncertainty.

Since coming to power in 1997, the Labour government has frequently spoken of the need to build a new relationship between citizens and public services. There has certainly been a move to promote consultation and public involvement, a strategy which will be discussed in the next section, but there is little evidence of any strategy for changing the way that members of the public relate to the public agents engaged in frontline service delivery. The preceding discussion of what is required to build up trust highlights some of the issues that must be addressed if such a new relationship, one built on trust and mutual responsibility, is to be forged.

Public involvement and consultation

Over the past ten or fifteen years, opportunities for citizens to have their views on public service design and delivery heard have increased dramatically. The trend, started in large part by the Conservatives with the introduction of the Citizens' Charter, has resulted in a variety of different democratic tools being used to involve or consult citizens at all levels of government. There are a number of reasons for allowing citizens such input in the democratic process, which would include:

- Civic duty: the ideal of citizenship expressed by civic republicans such as Rousseau or Aristotle assumes that direct rather than representative democratic participation in pursuit of the common good is a foundation of the good life.

- Better information: Laswell and Kaplan argued that by engaging citizens in the policy-making process, policy-makers could access better more relevant information about service users' needs and preferences. (Laswell and Kaplan 1950, cited in Clarke 2002)

- Better services: since Labour's election in 1997, the improvement of public services has been a central theme. The establishment of Public Service Agreements has placed public consultation at the heart of service reform.

- Greater accountability: public involvement strategies such as the 5000-strong People's Panel introduced in 1998 were seen as ways of showing that the government was a 'listening government', receptive to criticism and open to feedback.

To these four reasons, a fifth may be added: the building of trust. According to this argument, public involvement and consultation might be part of a larger strategy to change the relationship between service providers and citizens, with greater participation and more accountability helping to build trust and responsibility on both sides. This is certainly an ideal to which the government has given plenty of lipservice, but which, as the previous section argued, has yet to make any great impact on the ways that services are delivered on the frontline.

The experience of residents in the case study areas seemed decidedly mixed on this issue. Whilst there were good signs that local Area Co-ordination was using innovative and exciting methods to involve residents in the creation of a 'visioning' document for both Hillfields and Canley, several complaints were made about the way in which a local RSL had gone about its recent consultation process. Hillfields, in particular, seemed to have had both positive and negative experiences of public involvement. The development of a three-year plan for the area had been based on extensive local consultation, and implementation then ensured the involvement of local groups and professional stakeholders in WATCH. This whole process was preceded by a period of genuine capacity-building which helped residents develop the skills and confidence required to undertake this consultation effectively. More negatively, a recent consultation process had been undertaken with a view to consulting social housing tenants on their opinions about the future of the tower blocks. Although this was always going to be a sensitive subject, several residents expressed bitter feelings both about the way the consultation took place and the likelihood that the towers would be knocked down whatever their views.

The latter example is important because it highlights one of the dangers of public involvement, namely that it raises expectations that participants' opinions will then dictate the outcome. This is rarely the case, and when it is (as in ballots for transfer of housing stock), the involvement strategy must be designed accordingly. That people may be disappointed by the outcome of a public involvement strategy is no reason not to pursue such direct democratic processes, but it is a very good reason to proceed with caution and to ensure that the process is designed and implemented appropriately. As another IPPR author has recently commented, 'we are of the belief that no public involvement is better than bad public involvement. In local government there are still too many poor quality attempts to involve the public. These have the effect of undermining the idea of involvement as a means for improving the quality of decision-making or reconnecting the public with civic and political life' (Clarke 2002).

In areas such as Canley, where levels of trust in authority are already low, it is essential that residents are involved in decision-making processes in some way. But it is equally essential that the parameters and limits of that involvement are always made clear, and that hopes are not unfairly raised. It would, of course, be ideal if some sort of bottom-up force for regeneration could come to act as an intermediary between the

Council and local residents, just as WATCH has in Hillfields. Without the existence of such a body, public involvement and consultation will remain a difficult but necessary strategy to pursue.

This points to the need for careful design of any processes for 'community engagement' in local planning and decision-making. There is a mass of evidence and expertise in the emerging field of facilitated consensus-building and participatory community development on which local authorities and other agencies can draw (Warburton 2000; Warburton 2001). Key lessons from this body of experience are that policy makers often confuse different levels of citizen 'involvement', leading to damaging mismatches between what local people think they can help achieve and what decision-makers are actually offering. As local authorities begin to establish their approaches to community planning and new initiatives to devolve some decision-making to neighbourhood or area level, it is vital that the lessons of good and bad practice in community involvement are learned and applied effectively. There is also a need to expand the provision of 'capacity-building' services to give local community groups the resources, knowledge and skills they need to participate effectively in local planning. Bodies such as WATCH need access to expanded provision of courses such as Common Purpose programmes (see Chapter 4) which are currently the preserve of professionals from the public, private and voluntary sectors; and there needs to be more formal recognition of the skills and knowledge built up by community groups in local regeneration and 'visioning' projects.

Political representatives

> *One councillor said that people in Canley are happy, they don't have any complaints...I said it is because people don't feel listened to.* (Long-term resident, Canley)

> *When we first moved in here, Dave Nellist turned up and knocked on the door. It felt like a very personal thing to do.* (New resident, Hillfields)

As stated in the introduction, Hillfields residents showed a surprising degree of trust in their political representatives. People we questioned in the other two areas studied were far more cynical about the value of their political representatives, and none of the residents in the Earlsdon focus groups could even name their councillors. Such negative views are actually very common. Local democracy itself is often portrayed as suffering a crisis of legitimacy with electoral turnout at local elections recently very low. What is remarkable then is not the extent of residents' disaffection with their councillors in Earlsdon or Canley, but rather the levels of approval and trust displayed by several of the Hillfields respondents.

A combination of two factors appeared to make a difference in Hillfields. First and most important, councillors such as Dave Nellist and Karen McKay are seen as open, approachable and accessible. People commented that they would take or return your call at almost any time of the day, that they would listen to residents' concerns and act on them and that they went out of their way to make themselves known even to new residents. The second factor which people referred to was the commitment these councillors showed towards the area. Again, this is not to say that councillors in other areas are not so committed, but rather to note that residents' perceptions in the three areas differ. One reason we were given for this was the party background of the councillors concerned. Nellist and McKay are candidates for the Socialist Alliance. Although they may be driven by a strong political ideology, neither have a large-scale national party which will direct their position on issues, nor are they seen to harbour personal ambitions to become members of Parliament or government. The perception of residents, at least, is that these individuals are more effective political representatives because the local community is their power base and their primary political concern. As noted above, there is a potential problem of an 'empathy gap' between residents and decision-makers and service providers who live in distant suburbs and have no personal stake in or regular contact with the lives of the communities they affect most; Nellist and McKay's success underlines the importance of closing such a gap.

Although these observations are the result of just a few conversations with local residents, there are principles at stake here which are worth highlighting. The first is the importance, once again, of local knowledge and empathy. Councillors were not generally seen by residents to manifest this, and the very local presence of Hillfields' councillors helped reassure people that they would act in the locality's best interests. The second principle raised concerns the tension between party structures and local accountability. Residents seemed most to want representatives who would be motivated by their loyalty to the area and their concern for local residents. They were less trusting of representatives who they saw as 'self-serving' or ambitious to achieve power beyond the local level. This observation has unfortunate repercussions for local councillors representing the major parties, and suggests that they may have to work harder than most to retain their electorate's approval.

Recommendation

More research on the connection between local party structure and perceptions of representatives' legitimacy should be undertaken in order to help us understand what is needed both to stimulate effective local leadership and to re-engage voters in local democracy.

Some 'trust-busters' and builders

It was clear from speaking to residents and public officers in all three areas that there are some key factors which make it easier or harder to build up trust in governance. These are outlined below.

Trust-busters

Many of these reflect tougher structural limitations which cannot be altered overnight, but there are others which policy-makers might usefully take note of and act upon:

- Pervasive fatalism following many disappointments and long-term economic decline: as one resident put it, for some people winning the Lottery was seen as the only salvation, and that would be a passport out of the area.

- Broken promises: even though actual promises had probably never been made, many residents in Canley felt that they had been let down by public agents in the past.

- Split responsibilities: several residents complained that it was impossible to get action taken on certain issues where responsibility appeared to be split between two or more agencies. The transfer of housing stock has, for example, made it harder to keep alley-ways, verges and gardens clean, as this becomes the RSL's responsibility rather than something which the Council can act on as part of their daily cleansing duties.

- The unwillingness of some residents to take responsibility for the anti-social behaviour of youngsters, with 'passionate resistance', as one community worker put it, from some parents to attempts to intervene and challenge anti-social behaviour of children; this in turn made rough behaviour and low-level crime seem intractable to residents and the actions of police or public services seemed ineffectual.

- The perception that the officials with whom residents deal on a daily basis have little decision-making power or authority to effect change.

- The disillusionment and apathy fostered by the red tape, complexity and slowness of official regeneration initiatives, are seen as de-motivating for local people and a major reason for lack of trust. Local community workers feel alienated by top-down regeneration bureaucracy: 'if we are put off, as articulate and confident people, what is the impact on unconfident, badly off local single mothers?'.

Trust-builders

What can build up trust in a place like Canley, and then generate initiatives and relationships that strengthen community spirit? It seems clear that the area could gain from examining and learning from the experience of Hillfields, which could easily have declined seriously as a community. There are several features of organisations such as WATCH which are conducive to the development of trust by residents, and some of these could be applied to public agencies as well as bottom-up third sector organisations:

- Accountability to local people: as a community-led and -owned body WATCH and the networks that are under its umbrella demonstrate this almost to an extreme.

- Tangible successes: achieving even minor tangible results is very important, whether this be securing government and EU funds for regeneration or even just removing racist graffiti within 24 hours of it appearing.

- A positive and strongly articulated vision of the change or services required and easily communicable plans as to how that will be delivered.

- Long-term commitment to bottom-up action and involvement of residents in processes of decision-making where appropriate, accompanied by an effective communication strategy.

- Experience and commitment: whether service-deliverers or councillors, it is essential that local figures of authority have an obvious understanding of local issues and a clear determination to improve the area's prospects.

- Continuity of service: high turnover of staff in frontline service positions can make it much harder to build up a relationship of trust.

6. Mainstreaming a concern for community

Community: a mainstream word but not a mainstream activity

The UK is replete with initiatives, policy statements, organisations and indicators that are intended to support and build up 'community'. On the face of it, there is no need for a 'mainstreaming' of community as a policy concern. But the message from the Coventry case studies and a mass of other research and experience is that it is easy for policies to undermine and fail to support decent local community relations.

For all the myriad initiatives aimed at supporting community, top-down policy has for decades been undermining the conditions in which vigorous public life and good relationships of trust can thrive. Unwittingly, many policy measures have failed to support community and have in many cases gradually corroded it. For example:

- *Housing policy:* the development of 'monocultures' of housing over decades has reinforced segregation by income, class and race and has produced many estates that are deprived of ready access to essential community services; moreover, it now seems that providers of social housing often do no better than public sector landlords did in taking community development seriously, although there are important exceptions such as the Peabody Trust and Notting Hill Housing Trust.

- *Transport policy:* despite their social advantages, the domination of towns and cities by cars has eroded the scope for social life in the streets, and has placed barriers between parts of communities.

- *Crime policy:* the withdrawal of police from local beats, and the focus on serious crime, have led to an increase in many areas in low-level crime and residents' fear of their neighbourhoods; also we have little idea what to do about dysfunctional families and the havoc they do to themselves and localities – damage that has only recently been given the attention it deserves by policymakers.

- *Policy on public space:* the lack of joined-up action to enhance and maintain public spaces, and the loss of investment over the last two decades in parks, play spaces and youth facilities, have contributed to the decline in 'liveability' and trust in many areas (Worpole 1998; Greenhalgh and Worpole 1995).

- *Education policy:* the consequences of 'parental choice' are still unclear and there remain concerns as to whether it might create more segregation by class in the school system, or break the link between families and local schools at secondary level.

- *Jobs and organisational development:* changes in organisational policy and professional ethos seem to have led to more of a premium being placed on mobility between jobs and on a wide range of experience, rather than on long-term dedication to a career in a particular place.

- *Regeneration policy:* despite all the lip service paid to 'empowering the community', funding is not devolved to community-owned organisations but is still controlled by public agencies and subject to what is, to professionals and community residents alike, an alienating, over-complex and costly bureaucracy of monitoring and micro-management of outputs. Comprehensive Spending Reviews have consistently failed to delegate any funds to community-run organisations. Yet until more trust is shown in the grassroots, we cannot expect the grassroots to have more confidence in top-down authorities. Money and policy processes are too often a mystery to the communities which are most affected by them (Christie and Worpole, 2000).

- *Performance indicators and targets from central government:* as Onora O'Neill recently argued in the Reith Lectures, micro-management from Whitehall is corrosive of confidence and innovation among local service providers and can undermine people's trust in public services (O'Neill 2002). Key Performance Indicators and targets may be effective in specifying outputs, but 'better community' is an *outcome*, and not one capable of reductive measurement on the model favoured by target-obsessed ministers. In particular, performance indicators and targets give few or no incentives – least of all in funding – for collaboration between agencies. One police officer noted that health authorities were hard to bring into joint work on community safety and crime prevention – for example in relation to mental health – because of the lack of funding incentives and rewards in terms of indicators: 'they don't get doughnuts for it'.

Such developments tend to undermine attachment to place and the capacity of residents to develop healthy social relations within their areas and – for those in isolated deprived areas – important 'weak ties' beyond them. The point here is simple: 'community' is not integrated into the assessment of public policy as it should be, and it is all too easy for policy-making to weaken community bonds. Below we consider what changes can be made to 'mainstream' policy development to avoid this and to help build up community relations.

Avoiding harm

Before doing this, however, some important caveats must be entered. It is not our aim, nor do we think it possible, to 'restore' community relations as many imagine them to have been in earlier decades. The cohesive community of place cherished in memory and imagination might or might not have been a desirable thing. But, for certain, it is not something that can be restored even if we wished to do so. Proposals for 'mainstreaming community' cannot be about the restoration of community of place to its once primary position in the formation of identity and the development of social bonds and roles. What it can be about, as Diane Warburton has suggested, is an *aspiration* for good local relationships and attitudes to the local shared environment (Warburton 1998).

Nor can we be too ambitious about what the 'mainstreaming' of a focus on community relations might achieve. So many structural factors are also at work – above all, the operations of the economy, class and accumulated patterns of advantage and deprivation that we cannot expect to transform local social relationships overnight. Policies aimed at reducing poverty, improving health and education, fighting crime, and improving public transport will all take decades to work through, and will make major contributions over the long run to the conditions that influence the quality of local community relations. But although we need to be suitably modest about the impact of action to support community, it is nonetheless important to the quality of life for residents. At the very least, mainstreaming of concern for community relationships can help reinforce the first commandment of policy-making: *do no harm.* Using criteria of quality in local community relations for testing policy ideas should at the minimum help alert decision-makers and service providers to the scope for new measures to do damage inadvertently to the local ecology of relationships. While it is much harder to devise policies that actively foster better relations between residents, avoiding harm is the starting point.

Against this backdrop, we believe the policy proposals made in the previous chapters can make a positive difference. They are not radical departures from existing policy frameworks; but they do make sharp points about the need to put the principles of community-building within these frameworks into practice, and to remove barriers to doing this.

Community counts: using the policy frameworks we have

Progress is being made in developing policy frameworks and processes that in principle can integrate consideration for community relationships more effectively into policy, both as a means of avoiding harm to them, and as a way of seeking to improve them or at least provide the conditions for improvement. It is worth listing some of those initiatives or policy-making frameworks which might easily come to incorporate a more explicit concern to support community.

Sustainable development should be the guiding framework

At the national, regional and local levels, the adoption (in theory at least) of principles of sustainable development stands as the most obviously appropriate framework for community-sensitive policy-making. This is a model of development that seeks to integrate environmental, social and economic issues and produce policies that recognise the interconnection and interdependence of all these domains. Policy-making that supports community, should, by extension, take sustainable development seriously. It should entrench environmental issues and social equity in economic decision-making, and recognise the connections between economic and social deprivation and environmental degradation (Warburton 1998; Worpole 2000b). Sustainability appraisal tools are coming into use across the planning system and in the development of regional and local strategic plans. Indicators and 'impact assessment' tools for measuring the state of community relations need to be developed within the context of sustainable development both as a goal and a framework for appraisal.

Community strategies

The advent of Community Planning as a key element in the modernisation of local government should also help produce more joined-up policy development and delivery of services. Community strategies should be devised in partnership with all sectors of the community by local councils, and councils now have a power of pursuing the long-term 'well-being' of their communities. The modernisation of local government should also contribute to better connections between top-down policy from councils and other agencies and bottom-up community-led initiatives.

Joining up government initiatives

There are several crosscutting departments within government which have a remit to support community. The most important of these are the Active Communities Unit in the Home Office, the Neighbourhood Renewal Unit and the Community Cohesion Unit. There is a clear opportunity and need to ensure effective 'joining up' between these units and thinking elsewhere in government (for example, the Cabinet Office Strategy Unit, which is looking at social capital, geographic mobility and other themes relevant to community relations). These departments could also lead by example in communicating the message that community matters for everyone, not just those in deprived areas. 'Community' can easily become shorthand for 'a deprived neighbourhood', but good community relations and the responsibilities that they demand are relevant to all (Christie and Worpole 2001). In this context, more discussion from politicians of the need for the affluent to take community seriously and to have common cause with the worse-off is important.

Making neighbourhood renewal work for community

Government is putting substantial funds into the worst-off neighbourhoods via the Neighbourhood Renewal Unit (NRU) and Local Strategic Partnerships. The Neighbourhood Renewal Fund and Strategy aim at achieving 'floor targets' in health, education, crime reduction, employment, housing and environmental protection. These policy goals are all fundamental to achieving the conditions in which community relationships can flourish, and to the improvement of trust between residents and the public agencies working with them. New models of 'neighbourhood management' – such as introduction of neighbourhood wardens – and proposals for 'mainstreaming' of measures for improving the well-being of the worst-off places are in development.

The NRU is also promoting not just *outcomes*, but also *processes* which will support healthy community relationships, such as partnership working, empowerment of residents to collaborate in decision-making and creation of mutually reinforcing initiatives and funding streams. Much remains to be done to put all this into practice, but there is at least a high-level understanding in the NRU of the need for genuine measures to foster community of place and catalyse action by residents. The NRU is now exploring better ways to engage people from its target communities in consultations about spending priorities, so that a network of community representatives can be in place for the next Comprehensive Spending Review in 2004. However, much more should be done to devolve not just *a say in spending* but also *some funds* fully to mutual or co-operative community-led groups that have proved their 'capacity', such as WATCH in Hillfields, for management and improvement of public spaces and parks, for example, or for development of facilities for young people. The Neighbourhood Renewal Fund should include provision for this as a pilot in full financial devolution and genuine 'empowerment' of communities.

Consultation and performance measures

More local authorities and the Audit Commission are exploring ways to improve community consultations and participatory initiatives involving residents of local areas, and developing indicators of community 'engagement'. The development of better local strategies for consultation and participation should help to overcome problems of 'consultation fatigue' or the poorly targeted and implemented efforts at 'engaging with the community', which often lead to criticisms from residents when great efforts in consultation lead to total lack of follow-up action (Warburton 2000). But these measures need to be accompanied by major changes in the regime of performance indicators and targets imposed on local authorities and other agencies by the Government. While the Audit Commission has reduced significantly the number of targets imposed on councils, little has been done to address the distortions introduced by targets and rigid performance indicators tied to inputs and outputs. The way forward is to reduce the Whitehall indicator set radically, to allow agencies and services to be judged far more on *outcomes* and to do this by assessing their performance against the *experiences* of service users, peers among local agencies, and residents in disadvantaged communities. Moreover, we need to see the development of performance measures that reward and encourage joined-up action between agencies and work on local partnerships: work that is marginalised and constrained by the pressure of fitting it in to the few gaps available in the mainstream activity of meeting targets.

Measuring 'community': it can be done

The New Economics Foundation has been researching innovative methods for assessing the impact on community relations of regeneration activities (Walker *et al*, 2001). The 'Prove It!' methodology is a way of evaluating the benefits of projects for their effect on the local social environment, such as changes wrought in people's perceptions of their neighbours and strangers, or their feelings of confidence in taking civic action locally. Crucially, it has been shown that the very act of measurement actually builds social capital as residents are themselves necessarily engaged in the process of evaluation. The methodology, supported by Groundwork and Barclays Bank is being refined and extended and offers a promising and innovative way forward for locally-based assessment of regeneration programmes' impacts on community spirit.

Business and community: new pressures

Pressure is mounting for big businesses to be obliged to report publicly on their involvement in, and impact on, local communities, and many companies already produce a 'social impact' study as part of their corporate social responsibility agenda. Such a requirement could be a catalyst for much wider use of 'soft tools' such as the Prove It! methodology and for close attention by corporations to the impact of their activities on community – whether negative or positive. Developers, for example, are being brought formally into a community impact assessment process in London. Under the revised London Plan, developers in London are now expected to assess how proposals for new property developments will assist councils in meeting the floor targets for neighbourhood renewal, and to examine the impact of proposals on communities at the earliest design stage.

Planning and community

Linked to the latter point, the review of the planning system has produced calls from the Government for developers to consult more effectively with communities before tabling proposals for new development. But a more joined-up approach is still required and the review of planning now in hand is a potentially valuable catalyst for this. As the planning system is reformed, there is scope for far better integration between land use planning, community strategies, participatory techniques for community involvement in decisions, and neighbourhood renewal schemes. All need to be seen as connected processes within a coherent national framework for sustainable development at all levels (Christie, Walker and Warburton 2002).

There is thus no shortage of policy initiatives or approaches which could help to support community. The clear priority is to join them up effectively, avoid contradictions and incoherence, and work within a clear strategic framework. That framework already exists – the overarching goals and criteria of sustainable development – but the joining up needs to be continuously improved, with the Government simplifying the diverse units and initiatives wherever possible to reduce the risk of clashing objectives, confusion, frustration, red tape and reinvention of wheels. But such a framework cannot alone secure better attention to community relations in the design of policies. We also need some simple and effective tools for assessing policies. The next sections outline the case for a community-proofing process.

Supporting community? Assessing the impact of policy

Preceding chapters have outlined the reasons why an 'early warning system' is needed in policy-making to assess the potential damage to community relations from new proposals, and to improve the scope for better community links at the design stage. Such a system could adopt either of two forms: firstly we could seek to assess the effect of policies on community after their implementation, or we could endeavour to 'community-proof' policies before implementation at the design stage.

Measuring community: impacts and indicators

A great deal of effort has been put into development of indicators of local services and local government performance in recent years, and many initiatives have been launched to attempt to find measures for ideas such as 'community', 'quality of life' and 'sustainability'. For example, the Audit Commission and IDeA have set up a Local Indicators Project, seeking to devise measures of community involvement in decision-making. The aim of such indicators is to determine whether or not policies are working or achieving the results they were hoped to attain, in this case by assessing whether residents are effectively engaged in local processes of decision-making. Very often, though, indicators are used to measure not outcomes (end-states such as a better-educated workforce) but outputs (such as number of students attaining 'A' levels in any one year) and these inevitably only provide a snapshot of the full picture. Could we, in the spirit of accountable and evidence-based policy-making, find indicators which would capture either the outputs or outcomes of policies that relate to local community relations?

A paper commissioned for IPPR on measuring community outcomes underlined the difficulties thrown up by such projects for capturing complex sets of relationships and interactions in quantifiable indicators (Bennett 2002). The problems and challenges include:

- The difficulties of finding appropriate measures: we need to be sure that the indicators chosen are fit for purpose, not simply convenient for measurement and comparison.

- Identifying factors that connect inputs to outcomes: a task that is especially difficult in relation to the quite personal 'feel' of 'community'.

- Controlling the costs of data collection and auditing.

- The reluctance of local authorities and other actors to be given yet more indicators of performance and demands for evaluation.

- The problem of top-down imposition of indicators on communities: Prove it! methodology of participatory approaches shows the benefits of involving local people but on the other hand, community-owned indicator sets may mean very limited scope for comparison across areas.

- The need for indicators to contain a 'bias for action', prompting some agency to do something in response to the information they convey. To be avoided at all costs is a culture of 'box-ticking' that leads to no action on the matters being measured.

- The danger that agencies will use the indicators that are easiest to collect, whereas in the worst-off areas the key measures are typically the hardest to get hold of, such as information on domestic violence, access to drugs or the informal economy.

- The risk of adding to 'consultation overload' in many areas if a new process is introduced for assessing how the local community is working.

Added to this list of concerns there are two final problems that make the idea of testing policies after implementation very unattractive. Preceding chapters have already discussed the effect of an indicator-driven professional culture. Targets do not help public authorities react effectively to immediate local issues, and they can encourage the tendency to 'miss seeing the wood for the trees'. Secondly, we have sought to emphasise the extent to which key structural factors such as poverty and polarisation of wealth can inhibit the capacity of policy-makers to alter local community relations. Given that there are already so many performance indicators which local authorities and public services are bound by, it seems rather unfair to burden them with yet another set for which they can only be seen as partially responsible.

Catching problems at the design stage

Rather than trying to measure the impact of policies on community after they are implemented, the alternative would be to try and build in safeguards to the process of policy design itself. Is there scope for use of a standard toolkit for community-proofing by all the diverse agencies that could gain value from it, such as developers, councils, public agencies, regeneration partnerships, community groups? In the course of our case studies, seminars and interviews, we tested this idea.

The challenge was to identify the beneficial features of 'community' and use them in a 'community-proofing tool': a framework of criteria to help policy makers assess, at the design stage of local initiatives in different areas of policy, what they need to consider in relation to the impact of their proposals on community cohesion and bonds. The tool would use criteria based on the answers that flow from key questions to residents, such as: What makes people feel that 'community' is weakening? What are the factors that they see as contributing to improvements in their neighbourhood and community relationships?

Certainly this idea begs many questions. Exactly what kinds of community, social capital or community cohesion are desirable, and which do we want to avoid? And even if we think we know what kinds of community we want to foster, can we actually identify them in practical terms for policy purposes? Can we identify criteria that would help us to check in advance whether a policy will have a positive or negative effect on community relations? Amongst the key difficulties we would anticipate arising with a community-proofing approach would be:

- Finding the right criteria could prove difficult. It is not clear that there are general 'rules' about the sorts of actions which have a supportive or damaging effect on community.

- It might be hard in practice to distinguish between 'inclusive' and 'exclusive' elements of communities. The issue of faith-based schools poses the problem in sharp focus: on the one hand, they seem to be associated with many 'community virtues', while on the other they are, by definition, exclusive.

- Community-proofing could have little to say about the way in which policies are implemented. Even the most apparently community-friendly policies at the design stage could potentially be implemented in such a way as to actually damage local social ties.

- Community-proofing and any resulting consultation could simply add to the 'consultation overload' experienced in many areas.

- Indicators and criteria cannot prevent there being conflicts between certain goals in community development. However, a community-proofing process could help highlight such conflicts at the design stage and prompt action to resolve them or minimise them.

Community-proofing: a modest proposal

We acknowledge all these difficulties. The way ahead we propose is suitably modest and experimental: to develop a community-proofing tool as a form of guidance for the design stage of national, regional and local policies, setting out key criteria and questions to be taken fully into account when policies are devised. The aim would be two-fold:

- to alert policy makers to the potential for improving local community relationships;

- to highlight the risks of inadvertently damaging local social capital and community cohesion.

Together these goals would contribute to the *mainstreaming* of concern for local community relations in policymaking. If carefully designed and implemented there is no reason why many of the problems outlined above could not be effectively resolved.

The tool would be based on what can be learned from the research literature and our experience about what erodes, and what builds, community. As preceding chapters have shown, whilst there may not be hard and fast rules as to what factors support or undermine community, we do have experience of factors which generally seem to have positive or negative effects. This would give us the basis of an initially rather 'blunt' tool, but the criteria used would be open to refinement and debate. Necessarily the tool would take a minimalist approach to community, drawing on criteria for assessment of effects that could be applied to *any* type of neighbourhood – affluent or disadvantaged – in the country.

Community-proofing would not be a post-hoc evaluation method but rather a *preventive* and *deliberative* process to be applied at the earliest design stage of policy-making, and forming part of a general framework of policy for sustainable development. This is all-important and reflects the principles of, and lessons from, the use of sustainability appraisal and environmental assessment methods. The use of a community-proofing process should be seen as integral to, not distinct from, processes for appraising and ensuring the compatibility of policies with the goals of sustainable development (DETR 1999). It would be integrated with the development of community strategies and local planning frameworks at local authority level; with regional sustainable development frameworks at the regional level; and with Departmental processes for sustainability appraisal of policies. If so integrated, the burden of consultation should not be increased, and importantly it would be a process that itself could produce beneficial effects for social capital, as we envisage it being used in conjunction with participatory approaches to local decision-making.

Users would start from the modest premise of *avoiding harm*, and should be suitably wary of claiming to be able to design policies that would certainly improve community relations. The tool would not be yet another indicator set, but would instead be a process for 'joining up' policy issues and focusing attention on potential unintended consequences. The tool's capacity to expose policy trade-offs between goals of community and other aims should, in this light, be regarded as a strength rather than a weakness.

The tool would be useful for both local and national government, but could also be applied by companies, community groups, even classes of schoolchildren as part of their citizenship education programme. It could be applied in contexts such as:

- Regeneration programme and project planning;

- Development of community strategies;

- Proposals for new facilities, such as development of faith-based schools in an area;

- Development planning, as a means of minimising disputes over siting;

- Design of new housing developments.

How community-proofing might work

The community-proofing tool would be a *process of deliberation*, undertaken wherever possible in a participatory way with involvement of local residents in order to capture in a rich way all the local knowledge about social networks that conventional measurement systems miss. It would call decision-makers' attention early in a policy-making procedure to the possible effects of decisions on the quality of community relations. Drawing on the literature and the experience of the Coventry case studies, there are three components of community which policy-makers might work to protect:

- A rich variety of 'weak' and 'strong' ties locally;

- Trust and civility, required to maintain or produce a 'reassuring' community and 'liveable' environment;

- A sense of local pride and identity, while avoiding an 'enclave' mentality.

Under each of these themes, several criteria could be offered against which a policy or proposal could be tested. These criteria would be based on the factors that through research and experience, we know to have positive or negative effects on community. The work undertaken in Coventry suggested the following structure:

- To ascertain whether the proposal would support or undermine a rich variety of social ties:
  - Would the proposal erode local spaces and places for congregation or interaction?
  - Would the proposal discourage the development of community action networks?
  - Would the proposal erect physical barriers to interaction between different local social groups?
  - Would it create social and cultural barriers to interaction?

- To ascertain whether the proposal would support or undermine trust and civility:
  - Would the proposal create or establish social and cultural monocultures?
  - Would it foster resentment and conflict between communities?
  - Would the proposal encourage crime and anti-social behaviour?
  - Would it undermine the quality of the streetscape?

- To ascertain whether the proposal would support or undermine local pride and identity:
  - Would the proposal destroy local landmarks positively associated with the community?
  - Would the proposal encourage stigmatisation of the area?
  - Would the proposal reduce the quality of the local built and green environment?

In each case, supporting methods could be used, such as the approach developed by the Countryside Agency, *Quality of Life Capital*, a method that requires comprehensive listing of all the benefits and services provided by particular local assets (a building, forest, park etc) that are intended to be replaced or redeveloped, and a listing of the benefits and services expected to flow from the new development. This approach similarly requires careful assessment at the *design* stage of any policy of the risks of losing important assets that are hard to quantify, and of the scope for replacing them or avoiding their loss by rethinking the planned policy. (See www.countryside.gov.uk.)

The process would be compatible with other existing approaches to policy appraisal within a framework of sustainable development – such as 'rural proofing' of policies for their effect on communities in the countryside – and with community-based processes for local involvement in decision-making and in long-term planning (such as local 'visioning' initiatives). It would also be a contribution to more joined-up working across professional boundaries, as the process would force consideration of potential problems and avoidable risks to community relations, which would otherwise show up only in the experience of residents and the eventual evaluations done by service providers.

How might this work? We would envisage a variety of approaches to putting the process into practice, but in all cases there would be a period of deliberation built into the planning of a policy or development affecting a particular place; this process would be labelled 'community-proofing' and guided by independent facilitators who would be locally based, ideally, but not identified either with public policymakers or with the community interests most affected. The process could be based on an exhaustive round of working through questions raised by the community-proofing criteria listed above; or on more informal and creative processes, perhaps involving the creation of scenarios for the area based on different answers to the questions posed by the community-proofing framework. What these approaches to the process would have in common is the aim of making explicit – bringing to the surface – many of the qualitative aspects of community relations that would simply not be captured otherwise, and then prompting reflection on how proposals could be changed in order to avoid unintended harm to community qualities. The process would also highlight trade-offs in situations where the policy does not score well according to the community-proofing criteria, but where other policy goals might just be deemed more important.

Recommendation

We recommend that this community-proofing approach be refined further in a series of pilots, to be undertaken in a variety of communities, affluent and less well-off, by a range of organisations such as:

- Local authorities, in developing community plans and integrating strategies for open space with policies for regeneration, transport, education and leisure;
- Neighbourhood renewal partnerships, in developing regeneration programmes and projects;
- Property developers and planners, in assessing the impact and drawing up the design of proposed new housing developments;
- Local Strategic Partnerships, in assessing long-term scenarios arising from diverse visions of how their areas could develop;
- Faith communities, in assessing proposals for the introduction of faith-based schools.

The community-proofing approach recommended here is no panacea, of course. It cannot begin to tackle the structural problems that condemn many areas to long-term poverty, crime, low educational attainment, and so on. Nor can it make people interact when they have no interest in doing so, or guarantee that people will be better members of their community.

But what it *can* do is valuable, by alerting decision-makers to issues all too often overlooked in the design phase of policymaking and physical development. In many ways, the process of community-proofing would simply be a way of ensuring that policy-makers exercise 'common-sense' when thinking about the likely effects of a policy. All the criteria included in the model outlined above are really quite obvious comments on what is and is not helpful in supporting a vigorous public life and the conditions in which trust will thrive. If the references to 'deliberation', 'consultation' and 'facilitators' sound off-putting, then it is worth simply looking at the community-proofing tool as a way of reminding policy-makers that community matters and that they can help or hinder that process in fairly clear-cut ways.

Community-proofing could have made it plain to decision-makers that there would be adverse impacts on community from, for example, the run-down in budgets for the maintenance of public parks, highlighting the false economy of such neglect of the public realm. It could have helped make clear the adverse effects of the neglect of staffing and maintenance of tower blocks. It could have made clear the impacts of concentrating badly-off households in housing estates remote from key services and deprived of good congregational facilities. We have paid a high price collectively for these mistakes, and the worst-off and most vulnerable have paid the heaviest price of all. Community-proofing could not have prevented all such mistakes, but it could have made plain the full range of risks being run, and given pause for reflection and redesign of policies at an early stage.

What parallels exist in 2002? Community-proofing of proposals for faith-based schools would be well-advised given the risks of social and cultural divisiveness; and would be a valuable technique to pilot in relation to the proposed multi-faith school in Westminster. The plans for building hundreds of thousands of new homes in the South East in coming years demand very careful community-proofing, in case we produce a new generation of rootless, monotonous, disconnected estates where community ties have been neglected and communal spaces and facilities treated as an after-thought. These two examples should make it clear that the stakes are high: we need to put far more thought now into the design of new policies and developments than we did in the past.

Conclusion

'Community' is a slippery term, perhaps the most easily abused in the social science and political lexicons. The risks, in appealing to ideas of 'community cohesion' and 'community identity', of falling into nostalgia, sentimentality and unrealistic hopes, are obvious. In this report we have focused on one dimension of 'community': social relations in particular places. It can be argued that this aspect of community has declined, is declining and could be eclipsed by new forms of social bonding in communities of choice and interest. But community of place counts still, and for some it matters a great deal. We notice it most when it begins to decay because no matter how rich our dispersed communities of interest might be, we still need to feel reassured about the place in which we live, and we need to be able to offer reassurance to strangers who come into it. The growing importance of 'liveability' to government policy-makers, and the establishment of the Neighbourhood Renewal Unit, testify to the new understanding of how place matters to quality of life. We have argued that we can build up a rich and coherent approach to community of place, drawing on the experience of three diverse communities in Coventry and on the large research literature; and that this can and should be applied to policy making.

The key lesson is that while large structural forces in the economy and society profoundly affect what people want and are enabled to do, small-scale decisions about the nature of the places in which they live, and about the ways in which they can come into contact with one another, make a vital difference to quality of community life. We need to be modest about what can be done to influence community relations in positive ways but we can do much better in avoiding damage to community of place, and in identifying early on in decision-making the questions we need to ask about the impact of policies and developments on the ties that bind us to one another and to places.

This report has used the experience of three very different neighbourhoods to highlight the various ways in which public policy can have a significant effect on the quality of local social relations. Although the different circumstances of each locality should show that the impact of a policy will differ according to the way that it is implemented in any one place, several key policy areas have been shown to have a particularly important effect. Those policy areas are:

- Planning and development

- Provision for young people

- Crime reduction and policing

- Design and liveability of the public realm

- Methods of frontline service delivery.

If public policy is to support rather than undermine community of place then it is essential that policy-making in these areas be particularly sensitive to its impact on local social relations. Although there may be powerful structural factors which limit the potential of community to thrive in any one area, if every effort is made to get policy thinking 'right' on the issues listed above, then a suitable framework will have been put in place within which community might have some chance of developing.

Many recommendations have been made over the course of this report, in what might seem to be a fairly piecemeal approach. It is important to note, though, that whilst these recommendations identify policy areas where clear improvements could be made, they are really just examples of what a more community-sensitive approach might require. In order for policy to support community, it is vital that a concern for community is built into the very nature of policy conceptualisation and design. In the same way that liberal policy-making is largely driven by a set of values that could include fairness, equity, efficiency and efficacy, so community might be added to that list. It should just be common sense that policies which destroy opportunities for interaction, or which make neighbourhoods less rather than more reassuring, will also destroy the foundations of cohesion and community. Identifying which policies have such an effect is where some careful thinking is required.

Whilst it is far harder for policy-makers to aspire to positively nurture and nourish community relations, the community-proofing tool presented in the last chapter at least suggests a way in which the tenet of 'do no harm' could be respected. Such a tool provides policy-makers with a way of identifying which policies might undermine community, and so enables trade-offs to be made between possibly conflicting policy goals. Even if public policy cannot make people interact or trust each other, it can provide or destroy the conditions within which interaction and trust become possible, and this is what we have sought to highlight in the fore-going report. We have set out a wide range of proposals for making this complex process more open, comprehensive and effective: from more exposure of decision-makers to the people and places their policies influence, to the use of community-proofing to assess the possible effects of policies. Taken together, these can help us create more sustainable, cohesive and reassuring communities of place.

References

Appleyard D, Gerson M and Lintell M (1981) *Liveable Streets* Berkeley: University of California Press

Armitage R (2002) *To CCTV or Not To CCTV?* available at www.nacro.org.uk/publications/index.htm

Aronson E, Blaney N, Stephan C, Sikes J and Snapp M (1978) *The Jigsaw Classroom* Beverley Hills: Sage

Atkinson R (2002) 'Does gentrification help or harm urban neighbourhoods?' available at www.neighbourhoodcentre.org.uk/research

Atkinson R and Kintrea K (1998) *Reconnecting Excluded Communities: the neighbourhood impacts of owner occupation* Edinburgh: Scottish Homes

Barton H (ed) (2000) *Sustainable Communities* London: Earthscan

Benn M (2000) 'A Short March Through the Institutions: Reflections on New Labour's Gender Machinery' in Coote A (2000) *New Gender Agenda* London: ippr

Bennett J (2002) *Measuring Community* unpublished seminar paper commissioned for ippr

Biddulph M (2002) *The Urban Village: a real or imagined contribution to sustainable development?* Cardiff: Cardiff University/ERSC

Blair T (2001) 'Improving Your Local Environment', speech given at Groundwork Conference, Croydon 24 April 2001

Blair T (2002) 'New Labour and Community' *Renewal 10.2* London: Lawrence & Wishart

Burkitt N (2001) *A Life's Work* London: ippr

CABE (2000) *By Design* Companion Guide to PPG1 London: DTLR

CABE (2002a) *Paving the Way: How we achieve safe, clean and attractive streets* London: CABE

CABE (2002b) *Streets of Shame* London: CABE

Christie I, Walker P and Warburton D (2002) *Putting Community at the Heart of Development* Reading: Green Issues Ltd

Christie I and Worpole K (2000) *Changing Places, Changing Lives: Sustainability and Modernisation on Solid Ground* Birmingham: Groundwork Federation

Christie I and Worpole K (2001) 'Quality of Life' in Harvey A (ed) *Transforming Britain* London: Fabian Society

Clarke R (2002) *New Democratic Processes* London: ippr

Coleman J (1988) *The Foundations of Social Theory* Massachusetts: Harvard University Press

Coventry City Council (2001) *Neighbourhood Renewal Fund Baseline of Priority Neighbourhoods for Years One and Two* Coventry

DETR (2001a) *Travel to Work* Transport Statistics Personal Travel Factsheet 3 – March 2001 www.transtat.dft.gov.uk/facts/ntsfacts/travwork/travwork.htm

DETR (2001b) *Travel to School* Transport Statistics Personal Travel Factsheet 2 – March 2001 www.transtat.dft.gov.uk/facts/ntsfacts/travscl/school01.htm

DETR (2000a) *Quality and Choice: A Decent Home for All* London: DETR

DETR (2000b) *Policy and Planning Guidance 3 on Housing* www.dtlr.gov.uk

DETR (1999) *A Better Quality of Life: a strategy for sustainable development for the UK* London: DETR

DfEE (2000) *Schools in England 2000* London DfES

DfES (2001) *Transforming Youth Work* consultation document London: DfES

DTLR (2002) *Green Spaces, Better Places* Final Report of the Urban Green Spaces Taskforce London: DTLR

Feinstein L (1998) 'Which Children Succeed and Why: What are the keys to success for British schoolchildren?' *New Economy* June 1998 5.2, cited in Hallgarten J (2000) *Parents Exist, OK?* London: ippr

Forrest R and Kearns A (1999) *Joined-Up Places? Social Cohesion and Neighbourhood Regeneration* York: Joseph Rowntree

Frazer E (2002) 'Local social relations: public, club and common goods' in Nash V (2002) *Reclaiming Community* London: ippr

Frazer E (1999) *The Problem with Communitarian Politics: unity and conflict* Oxford: OUP

Gaber I (2002) 'Every picture' in Guardian Society *The Guardian* 31 July

Goodman A (2002) *Inequality and Living Standards in Great Britain: Some Facts* Institute for Fiscal Studies Briefing paper 19 www.ifs.org.uk/inequality/bn19.pdf

Gorard S (2000) 'Size Matters: does school choice lead to spirals of decline?' Paper presented at the British Educational Research Association Annual Conference, Cardiff

Greenhalgh L and Worpole K (1995) *Park Life; urban parks and social renewal* London: Comedia/Demos

Gwilliam M *et al* (1998) *Sustainable Renewal of Suburban Areas* York: Joseph Rowntree Foundation

Hampton K and Wellman B (2000) 'Examining Community in the Digital Neighbourhood: Early Results from Canada's Wired Suburb' in Ishida T and Ibister K (eds) *Digital Cities: Technologies, Experiences & Future Perspectives* Heidelberg: Springer-Verlag

Health Education Authority (1999) *The Influence of Social Support and Social Capital on Health* London: Health Education Authority

Hogg MA and Abrams D (1988) *Social Identifications* London: Routledge

Holmans A (2001) *Past and Current Trends in House Prices and Incomes and Access to Home Ownership* Cambridge: Department of Land Economy

Home Office (2001a) *A Report of the Independent Review Team* (chaired by Ted Cantle) London: Home Office

Home Office (2001b) *Building Cohesive Communities: A Report of the Ministerial Group on Public Order and Community Cohesion* London: Home Office

Home Office (2001c) *Policing a New Century* London: Home Office

Hoyle C and Young R (2002) *Proceed With Caution: An evaluation of the Thames Valley Police Initiative in restorative cautioning* York: Joseph Rowntree Foundation

Jacobs J (1961) *The Death and Life of Great American Cities* (2000 edition) London: Pimlico

Jupp B (1999) *Living Together: Community Life on Mixed Tenure Estates* London: Demos

Lasswell HD and Kaplan A (1950) *Power and Society: A framework for political inquiry* New Haven: Yale University Press

Local Government Association (LGA) (2002) *Draft Guidance on Community Cohesion* (consultation document) London: LGA

Loxley C *et al* (2002) *Summer Splash Schemes 2000: findings from six case studies* London: Home Office

Miers D, Maguire M, Goldie S, Sharpe K, Hale C, Netten A, Uglow S, Doolin K, Hallam A, Enterkin J and Newburn T (2001) *An Exploratory Evaluation of Restorative Justice Schemes* London: Home Office

Miller N and Brewer MB (1984) *Groups in Contact: The Psychology of Desegregation* Orlando: Academic Press

MORI (2002) *Quality of Life Survey for the Audit Commission*

MORI (2000a) *Survey of service users for Best Value Pilot Areas* Survey for DTLR

MORI (2000b) *Surrey Childcare Audit Research* MORI & Surrey Early Years Development and Childcare Partnership

MORI (1998) *People's Panel survey for the Cabinet Office*

Mortimore P, Thomas S, Sammons P, Owen C and Pennell H (1994) *Assessing School Effectiveness: Developing measures to put school performance in context* London: Institute of Education

Nash V (ed) (2002) *Reclaiming Community* London: ippr

National Youth Agency (NYA) (2001) *Quality Develops: towards excellence in youth services* available at www.nya.org.uk

Neyroud P (2001) *Public Participation in Policing* London: ippr

Noden P (2001) 'School Choice and Polarisation: Any Evidence for Increased Segregation?' *New Economy 8.4* London: ippr

ODPM (2002) *Making the system work better – planning at regional and local levels* London: OPDM

ODPM (2002a) *Planning Policy Guidance 17* London: OPDM

Office for National Statistics (2001) Details to be found at www.statistics.gov.uk/socialcapital

O'Neill O (2002) *A Question of Trust* Reith Lectures 2002 London: BBC

Oswald A and Benito A (1999) *Commuting in Great Britain in the 1990s* working paper Department of Economics, Warwick University www.warwick.ac.uk/fac/soc/Economics/oswald/benito.pdf

Performance and Innovation Unit (2002) *Social Capital: A Discussion Paper* www.cabinet-office.gov.uk/innovation

Putnam R (2001) *Bowling Alone* New York: Simon & Schuster

Putnam R (1995) *Making Democracy Work* Princeton: Princeton University Press

Robson G and Butler T (2001) 'Coming to terms with London: middle-class communities in a global city' in *International Journal of Urban and Regional Research 25 (1)*

Rogers R and Power A (2000) *Cities for a Small Country* London: Faber & Faber

Sherif M, Harvey OJ, White BJ, Hood WR & Sherif CW (1961) *Inter-Group Conflict and Co-operation: the Robbers' Cave Experiment* Oklahoma: University of Oklahoma Book Exchange

Simmons J (2002) *Crime in England and Wales 2001/2002* London: Home Office

Social Exclusion Unit (2000a) *National Strategy for Neighbourhood Renewal: A framework for consultation* London: Stationery Office

Social Exclusion Unit (2000b) *Report of the Policy Action Team 11: Schools Plus* London: Stationery Office

Social Exclusion Unit (2000c) *Report of the Policy Action Team 12: Young People* London: Stationery Office

Social Exclusion Unit (2000d) *Report of the Policy Action Team 8: Anti-Social Behaviour* London: Stationery Office

Taylor M (2002) 'Community and Social Exclusion' in Nash V (ed) (2002) *Reclaiming Community* London: ippr

Urban Task Force (1999) *Towards an Urban Renaissance: Final report of the Urban Task Force* London: Stationery Office

Warburton D (2001) *Evaluating participatory, deliberative and co-operative ways of working* Brighton: Interact

Warburton D (ed) (2000) 'Planning and Participation' in a special section in *Town and Country Planning* May 2000

Warburton D (ed) (1998) *Community and Sustainable Development* London: Earthscan

WATCH (2002) *Community Consultation on the Hillfields Draft 10 Year Vision* Coventry: WATCH

Wellman B (1999) *Networks in the Global Village* Colorado: Westview Press

Wilson JQ and Kelling G (1982) 'Broken Windows' in *Atlantic Monthly* New York

Worpole K (2001) 'Renewal Starts at the Front Door' in *Regeneration and Renewal* 8 June

Worpole K (2000a) *Linking Home and School* London: Demos

Worpole K (2000b) *In Our Backyard: the social promise of environmentalism* London: Green Alliance

Worpole K (1998) *Nothing to Fear? Trust and respect in urban communities* London: Comedia/Demos

Young M and Wilmott P (1957) *Family and Kinship in East London* London: Routledge Kegan Paul

Young M and Wilmott P (1960) *Family and Class in a London Suburb* London: Routledge Kegan Paul

6 P (2001) *Profiles, networks, risk and hoarding: public policy and the dynamics of social mobility and social cohesion* unpublished paper presented at the PIU, Cabinet Office, London

Appendix

Methodology

The research was carried out in Coventry over the period of a year, with the support and interest of the City Council. Three areas were initially identified for study after a series of interviews with key local figures and visits to the areas themselves. Two of these areas (Earlsdon and Hillfields) are very geographically defined, and our study covered the whole of those neighbourhoods. Geographically, Canley covers a much less defined area, and as we were concerned to study only that part of it which might be classified as 'slipping' we actually studied a smaller area than would be demarcated as Canley on the map. We worked with the boundaries defined by the City Council's 'priority areas' classification, and notably, this classification did actually seem to match local residents' own perceptions of what counted as Canley.

In each of the three areas we carried out an ethnographic study, spending many days walking through each area, getting to know local features, local services and the character of the area. In order to understand the issues arising we interviewed a range of local stakeholders in each area[1], which included: community police officers, teachers, health workers, community and voluntary sector workers, youth workers, local businesses and Council officers.

As well as informally talking to local residents we also carried out focus groups to ascertain what residents themselves thought of the areas and the character of social relations there, and to determine whether our identification of key local issues was correct. We carried out two focus groups in each of the three neighbourhoods, one for established residents living there for more than five years, and one for relative newcomers of less than 18 months' residence. As far as possible each group was controlled to include a wide range of ages. Each group lasted for an hour and a half and had between eight and twelve respondents.

Two of the areas, Hillfields and Canley, proved too difficult to recruit for using standard market research techniques. In the end, local community groups were approached and agreed to recruit the groups from people known to them. This method of recruitment produces an element of self-selection and bias into the process. It is unlikely that those who attended the groups in both Hillfields and Canley are entirely typical of the wider populations of those two areas, probably most self-evident in their stated commitment to the area where they live. It is unlikely that the wider community would show similar levels of commitment and involvement, and this should be taken into account when reading the report. A full draft of the focus group report can be found at www.ippr.org.uk .[2]

The findings of this report will be communicated back to Coventry City Council with specific policy recommendations for each of the areas studied. A presentation will also be made to residents in the three areas.

Endnotes

1   Slightly fewer interviews were carried out in Earlsdon, largely because it proved harder to engage people in the research, perhaps because it is a more affluent area and there are therefore no over-arching bodies or networks which connect up all the relevant stakeholders.

2   This section of the methodology is taken from the introduction to the focus group report, written by Robin Clarke.